One
REFLECTION
a Day

AN INSPIRATIONAL
FIVE-YEAR JOURNAL

DAILY PROMPTS TO MEDITATE ON GOD'S WORD

Abigail R. Gehring

Good Books

New York, New York

Good Books books may be purchased in bulk at special discounts for sales promotion, corporate gifts, fund-raising, or educational purposes. Special editions can also be created to specifications. For details, contact the Special Sales Department, Good Books, 307 West 36th Street, 11th Floor, New York, NY 10018 or info@skyhorsepublishing.com.

Good Books is an imprint of Skyhorse Publishing, Inc.®, a Delaware corporation.

Visit our website at www.goodbooks.com.

10 9 8 7 6 5 4 3 2 1

Library of Congress Cataloging-in-Publication Data is available on file.

Cover design by Abigail Gehring

Print ISBN: 978-1-68099-644-9

Printed in China

How to Use This Book

For each day of the year, you'll find a Bible verse and a question or prompt. To get started, turn to today's date, fill in the year on the top line, read the verse and prompt, and then write your response in the lines provided. Don't worry about getting the answer "right"; just jot down your honest thoughts or feelings. And if a prompt doesn't resonate with you, feel free to simply meditate on the verse and write whatever comes to mind.

When you've completed a year, start the journal over using the next set of lines provided. As the years go by, you can glance back to see where you were at on that same day in previous years and how you may have grown or changed.

This is your journal. Use it however the Holy Spirit prompts you!

January

Be renewed in the spirit of your mind —*Ephesians 4:23 (KJV)*

How do you need the Holy Spirit to renew and refresh your mind as you start this new year?

20 _____ _____

_____

_____

_____

20 _____ _____

_____

_____

_____

20 _____ _____

_____

_____

_____

20 _____ _____

_____

_____

_____

20 _____ _____

_____

_____

_____

January

It is because of Yahweh's loving kindnesses that we are not consumed, because his compassion doesn't fail. —Lamentations 3:22 (WEB)

How have you experienced God's kindness and compassion lately?

20 _____ _____

_____

_____

_____

20 _____ _____

_____

_____

_____

20 _____ _____

_____

_____

_____

20 _____ _____

_____

_____

_____

20 _____ _____

_____

_____

_____

January

In the multitude of my thoughts within me thy comforts delight my soul. —Psalm 94:19 (KJV)

Are you delighting in God's goodness, or are you looking for other ways to calm, distract, or accept yourself?

20 _____ _____

_____

_____

20 _____ _____

_____

_____

20 _____ _____

_____

_____

20 _____ _____

_____

_____

20 _____ _____

_____

_____

_____

4

Then Peter came and said to him, "Lord, how often shall my brother sin against me, and I forgive him? Until seven times?"

Jesus said to him, "I don't tell you until seven times, but, until seventy times seven." —Matthew 18:21–22 (WEB)

Is there someone God is asking you to forgive?

20 _____ _____

_____

_____

_____

20 _____ _____

_____

_____

_____

20 _____ _____

_____

_____

_____

20 _____ _____

_____

_____

_____

20 _____ _____

_____

_____

_____

5

January

". . . When I called, no one answered; when I spoke, they didn't listen but they did that which was evil in my eyes, and chose that in which I didn't delight." —Isaiah 66:4 (WEB)

What is the Lord trying to show you or tell you today? How is He trying to draw you deeper into His delight?

20 _____ _____

_____

_____

20 _____ _____

_____

_____

20 _____ _____

_____

_____

20 _____ _____

_____

_____

20 _____ _____

_____

_____

January

6

We also rejoice in our sufferings, knowing that suffering produces perseverance; and perseverance, proven character; and proven character, hope: and hope doesn't disappoint us, because God's love has been poured into our hearts through the Holy Spirit who was given to us. —Romans 5:3–5 (WEB)

What hardship or suffering is in your life right now, and how is God's love influencing the way you experience it?

20 _____ _____

_____

_____

_____

20 _____ _____

_____

_____

_____

20 _____ _____

_____

_____

_____

20 _____ _____

_____

_____

_____

20 _____ _____

_____

_____

_____

January

For am I now seeking the favor of men, or of God? Or am I striving to please men? For if I were still pleasing men, I wouldn't be a servant of Christ. —Galatians 1:10 (WEB)

Are you getting a sense of worth—or worthlessness—from social media or certain people? What would it look like to let go of that and rest in the fact that God loves how He made you, and Jesus is enough to cover all the ways you fail?

20 _____ _____

_____

_____

20 _____ _____

_____

_____

20 _____ _____

_____

_____

20 _____ _____

_____

_____

20 _____ _____

_____

_____

January

8

Bear one another's burdens, and so fulfill the law of Christ.
—Galatians 6:2 (ESV)

How are you feeling about the people who are needing you or asking for your help?

20 _____ _____

_____

_____

_____

20 _____ _____

_____

_____

_____

20 _____ _____

_____

_____

_____

20 _____ _____

_____

_____

_____

20 _____ _____

_____

_____

_____

January

9

But Jesus beheld them, and said unto them, With men this is impossible; but with God all things are possible. —Matthew 19:26 (KJV)

What seemingly impossible thing are you praying for?

20 _____ _____

_____

_____

20 _____ _____

_____

_____

20 _____ _____

_____

_____

20 _____ _____

_____

_____

20 _____ _____

_____

_____

January

But they that wait upon the LORD shall renew their strength; they shall mount up with wings as eagles; they shall run, and not be weary; and they shall walk, and not faint. —Isaiah 40:31 (KJV)

What does it mean to wait upon the Lord?

20 ____ _____
_____
_____
_____

20 ____ _____
_____
_____
_____

20 ____ _____
_____
_____
_____

20 ____ _____
_____
_____
_____

20 ____ _____
_____
_____
_____

January

This is my comfort in my affliction, that your promise gives me life.
—Psalm 119:50 (ESV)

List some of God's promises.

20 _____ _____

_____

_____

20 _____ _____

_____

_____

20 _____ _____

_____

_____

20 _____ _____

_____

_____

20 _____ _____

_____

_____

January

"Therefore do not be anxious for tomorrow, for tomorrow will be anxious for itself. Sufficient for the day is its own trouble." —Matthew 6:34 (ESV)

What anxieties for the future can you trust God with today?

20 _____ _____

_____

_____

20 _____ _____

_____

_____

20 _____ _____

_____

_____

20 _____ _____

_____

_____

20 _____ _____

_____

_____

January

13

"For where your treasure is, there will your heart be also."
—Matthew 6:21 (KJV)

What do you treasure?

20 _____ _____

_____

_____

20 _____ _____

_____

_____

20 _____ _____

_____

_____

20 _____ _____

_____

_____

20 _____ _____

_____

_____

14

January

"Why do you see the speck that is in your brother's eye, but do not notice the log that is in your own eye?" —Matthew 7:3 (ESV)

Where do you need God's help to change your heart or your behaviors?

20 _____ _____

_____

_____

20 _____ _____

_____

_____

20 _____ _____

_____

_____

20 _____ _____

_____

_____

20 _____ _____

_____

_____

January

David said to Gad, "I am in deep distress. Let us fall into the hands of the Lord, for his mercy is great; but do not let me fall into human hands." —2 Samuel 24:14 (NIV)

What does God's mercy look like in your life right now?

20 _____ _____

_____

_____

20 _____ _____

_____

_____

_____

20 _____ _____

_____

_____

_____

20 _____ _____

_____

_____

_____

20 _____ _____

_____

_____

_____

16

January

For thou, LORD, hast made me glad through thy work: I will triumph in the works of thy hands. —Psalm 92:4 (KJV)

What good thing are you praising God for?

20 _____ _____

_____

_____

20 _____ _____

_____

_____

20 _____ _____

_____

_____

20 _____ _____

_____

_____

_____

20 _____ _____

_____

_____

_____

January

For the moment all discipline seems painful rather than pleasant, but later it yields the peaceful fruit of righteousness to those who have been trained by it. —Hebrews 12:11 (ESV)

How have you experienced God's discipline recently?

20 _____ _____

_____

_____

_____

20 _____ _____

_____

_____

_____

20 _____ _____

_____

_____

_____

20 _____ _____

_____

_____

_____

20 _____ _____

_____

_____

_____

January

18

Your eyes saw my unformed substance; in your book were written, every one of them, the days that were formed for me, when as yet there was none of them. —Psalm 139:16 (ESV)

Right now, how does it feel to remember that God is writing your story and knows how everything will work out?

20 _____ _____

_____

_____

_____

20 _____ _____

_____

_____

_____

20 _____ _____

_____

_____

_____

20 _____ _____

_____

_____

_____

20 _____ _____

_____

_____

_____

19

January

And he hath put a new song in my mouth, even praise unto our God: many shall see it, and fear, and shall trust in the Lord. —Psalm 40:3 (KJV)

Are you experiencing a joy that's so evident that it leads others to trust in the Lord?

20 _____ _____

_____

_____

_____

20 _____ _____

_____

_____

_____

20 _____ _____

_____

_____

_____

20 _____ _____

_____

_____

_____

20 _____ _____

_____

_____

_____

January

Be careful for nothing; but in every thing by prayer and supplication with thanksgiving let your requests be made known unto God. —Philippians 4:6 (KJV)

What are you anxious about?

20 _____ _____

_____

_____

_____

20 _____ _____

_____

_____

_____

20 _____ _____

_____

_____

_____

20 _____ _____

_____

_____

_____

20 _____ _____

_____

_____

_____

January

Be merciful unto me, O Lord: for I cry unto thee daily. —Psalm 86:3 (KJV)

Write a sentence or two to God expressing the pain or hardship you're experiencing.

20 ___ _____

_____

_____

20 ___ _____

_____

_____

_____

20 ___ _____

_____

_____

_____

20 ___ _____

_____

_____

_____

20 ___ _____

_____

_____

_____

January

Trust in the Lord with all thine heart; and lean not unto thine own understanding. —Proverbs 3:5 (KJV)

In what areas of your life or circumstances are you struggling to trust God?

20 _____ _____

_____

_____

_____

20 _____ _____

_____

_____

_____

20 _____ _____

_____

_____

_____

20 _____ _____

_____

_____

_____

20 _____ _____

_____

_____

_____

23

January

Show yourself in all respects to be a model of good works, and in your teaching show integrity, dignity, and sound speech that cannot be condemned . . . —Titus 2:7–8a (ESV)

In what ways might you need to repent and ask God to empower you with the Holy Spirit?

20 _____ _____

_____

_____

_____

20 _____ _____

_____

_____

_____

20 _____ _____

_____

_____

_____

20 _____ _____

_____

_____

_____

20 _____ _____

_____

_____

_____

24

January

Humble yourselves therefore under the mighty hand of God, that he may exalt you in due time . . . —1 Peter 5:6 (KJV)

In what areas might pride be creeping into your life?

20 _____ _____

_____

_____

_____

20 _____ _____

_____

_____

_____

20 _____ _____

_____

_____

_____

20 _____ _____

_____

_____

_____

20 _____ _____

_____

_____

_____

January

Then they cry unto the LORD in their trouble, and he saveth them out of their distresses. —Psalm 107:19 (KJV)

Use this space to cry out to the Lord about whatever is on your heart.

20 _____ _____

_____

_____

_____

20 _____ _____

_____

_____

_____

20 _____ _____

_____

_____

_____

20 _____ _____

_____

_____

_____

20 _____ _____

_____

_____

_____

January

When thou passest through the waters, I will be with thee; and through the rivers, they shall not overflow thee: when thou walkest through the fire, thou shalt not be burned; neither shall the flame kindle upon thee. —Isaiah 43:2 (KJV)

How have you experienced God's protection lately?

20 _____ _____

_____

_____

_____

20 _____ _____

_____

_____

_____

20 _____ _____

_____

_____

_____

20 _____ _____

_____

_____

_____

20 _____ _____

_____

_____

_____

January

Have not I commanded thee? Be strong and of a good courage; be not afraid, neither be thou dismayed: for the LORD thy God is with thee whithersoever thou goest. —Joshua 1:9 (KJV)

What are you facing that will require strength and courage?

20 _____ _____

_____

_____

20 _____ _____

_____

_____

_____

20 _____ _____

_____

_____

20 _____ _____

_____

_____

20 _____ _____

_____

_____

_____

January

Teach me good judgment and knowledge: for I have believed thy commandments. —Psalm 119:66 (KJV)

What situation are you facing that requires good judgment? Use this space to write a brief prayer.

20 _____ _____

_____

_____

_____

20 _____ _____

_____

_____

_____

20 _____ _____

_____

_____

_____

20 _____ _____

_____

_____

_____

20 _____ _____

_____

_____

_____

January

Yahweh's name is a strong tower: the righteous run to him, and are safe. —Proverbs 18:10 (WEB)

Where do you first turn for help with a problem—to God, or to things or people?

20 _____ _____

_____

_____

_____

20 _____ _____

_____

_____

_____

20 _____ _____

_____

_____

_____

20 _____ _____

_____

_____

_____

20 _____ _____

_____

_____

_____

January

While I live will I praise the LORD: I will sing praises unto my God while I have any being. —Psalm 146:2 (KJV)

What are you praising God for today?

20____ _____

_____

_____

_____

20____ _____

_____

_____

_____

20____ _____

_____

_____

_____

20____ _____

_____

_____

_____

20____ _____

_____

_____

_____

January

O keep my soul, and deliver me: let me not be ashamed; for I put my trust in thee. —Psalm 25:20 (KJV)

The psalmist is not shy about begging God for spiritual help ("keep my soul"), physical help ("deliver me"), and emotional help ("let me not be ashamed"), because he trusts God. Is there any area where you're holding back your prayers?

20 _____ _____

_____

_____

_____

20 _____ _____

_____

_____

_____

20 _____ _____

_____

_____

_____

20 _____ _____

_____

_____

_____

20 _____ _____

_____

_____

_____

February

In all thy ways acknowledge him, and he shall direct thy paths.
—Proverbs 3:6 (KJV)

Are there parts of your heart or your life where you're holding God at a distance, perhaps because you're afraid of change, or maybe you don't quite trust that God loves you and wants the best for you?

20 _____ _____

_____

_____

20 _____ _____

_____

_____

20 _____ _____

_____

_____

20 _____ _____

_____

_____

20 _____ _____

_____

_____

February

Blessed be God, even the Father of our Lord Jesus Christ, the Father of mercies, and the God of all comfort; Who comforteth us in all our tribulation, that we may be able to comfort them which are in any trouble, by the comfort wherewith we ourselves are comforted of God. —2 Corinthians 1:3–4 (KJV)

Who needs you to reach out with comforting or encouraging words today?

20 _____ _____

_____

_____

20 _____ _____

_____

_____

20 _____ _____

_____

_____

20 _____ _____

_____

_____

20 _____ _____

_____

_____

February

3

Come unto me, all ye that labour and are heavy laden, and I will give you rest. —Matthew 11:28 (KJV)

What burdens are weighing you down?

20 _____ _____

_____

_____

20 _____ _____

_____

_____

20 _____ _____

_____

_____

20 _____ _____

_____

_____

20 _____ _____

_____

_____

4

February

Fear thou not; for I am with thee: be not dismayed; for I am thy God: I will strengthen thee; yea, I will help thee; yea, I will uphold thee with the right hand of my righteousness. —Isaiah 41:10 (KJV)

What are you afraid of?

20 _____

20 _____

20 _____

20 _____

20 _____

February

5

Be of good courage, and he shall strengthen your heart, all ye that hope in the LORD. —Psalm 31:24 (KJV)

Write a brief prayer asking God for courage and strength for whatever you're facing today.

20 _____ _____

_____

_____

_____

20 _____ _____

_____

_____

_____

20 _____ _____

_____

_____

_____

20 _____ _____

_____

_____

_____

20 _____ _____

_____

_____

_____

February

And be ye kind one to another, tenderhearted, forgiving one another, even as God for Christ's sake hath forgiven you.
—Ephesians 4:32 (KJV)

Is there someone you need to forgive or ask forgiveness from?

20 _____ _____

_____

_____

_____

20 _____ _____

_____

_____

_____

20 _____ _____

_____

_____

_____

20 _____ _____

_____

_____

_____

20 _____ _____

_____

_____

_____

February

Peace I leave with you, my peace I give unto you: not as the world giveth, give I unto you. Let not your heart be troubled, neither let it be afraid. —John 14:27 (KJV)

In what ways are you seeking the world's peace instead of God's peace? What is the result?

20 _____ _____

_____

_____

_____

20 _____ _____

_____

_____

_____

20 _____ _____

_____

_____

_____

20 _____ _____

_____

_____

_____

20 _____ _____

_____

_____

_____

February

8

Restore unto me the joy of thy salvation; and uphold me with thy free spirit. —Psalm 51:12 (KJV)

Write a short prayer asking God to fill you with His joy.

20 _____ _____

_____

_____

_____

20 _____ _____

_____

_____

_____

20 _____ _____

_____

_____

_____

20 _____ _____

_____

_____

_____

20 _____ _____

_____

_____

_____

February

For I am persuaded, that neither death, nor life, nor angels, nor principalities, nor powers, nor things present, nor things to come, Nor height, nor depth, nor any other creature, shall be able to separate us from the love of God, which is in Christ Jesus our Lord.
—Romans 8:38–39 (KJV)

How might your day look different if you chose to rest in God's love rather than trying to earn it?

20 _____ _____

_____

_____

_____

20 _____ _____

_____

_____

_____

20 _____ _____

_____

_____

_____

20 _____ _____

_____

_____

_____

20 _____ _____

_____

_____

_____

February

Be still, and know that I am God: I will be exalted among the heathen, I will be exalted in the earth. —Psalm 46:10 (KJV)

Take a moment to be still and ask God to make Himself known to you in a fresh way. Write what you feel, jot down a Bible verse that comes to mind, or list some attributes of God that you've experienced or seen described in Scripture.

20 _____ _____

_____

_____

20 _____ _____

_____

_____

20 _____ _____

_____

_____

20 _____ _____

_____

_____

20 _____ _____

_____

_____

February

God is our refuge and strength, a very present help in trouble.
—Psalm 46:1 (KJV)

What do you need God's help with today?

20 _____ _____

_____

_____

_____

20 _____ _____

_____

_____

_____

20 _____ _____

_____

_____

_____

20 _____ _____

_____

_____

_____

20 _____ _____

_____

_____

_____

February

But thou, O LORD, art a shield for me; my glory, and the lifter up of mine head. —*Psalm 3:3 (KJV)*

Name some things or people you need God to shield you from.

20 _____ _____

_____

_____

20 _____ _____

_____

_____

20 _____ _____

_____

_____

20 _____ _____

_____

_____

20 _____ _____

_____

_____

February

Put on then, as God's chosen ones, holy and beloved, compassionate hearts, kindness, humility, meekness, and patience, bearing with one another and, if one has a complaint against another, forgiving each other; as the Lord has forgiven you, so you also must forgive. —Colossians 3:12–13 (ESV)

Write a brief prayer asking God to help you love someone who is difficult to love.

20 _____ _____

_____

_____

20 _____ _____

_____

_____

20 _____ _____

_____

_____

20 _____ _____

_____

_____

20 _____ _____

_____

_____

February

14

For God hath not given us the spirit of fear; but of power, and of love, and of a sound mind. —2 Timothy 1:7 (KJV)

In what way do you need the Holy Spirit's boldness in your life?

20____ _____

_____

_____

_____

20____ _____

_____

_____

_____

20____ _____

_____

_____

_____

20____ _____

_____

_____

_____

20____ _____

_____

_____

_____

February

I have set the LORD always before me: because he is at my right hand, I shall not be moved. —Psalm 16:8 (KJV)

Do you feel like God is front and center in your life, or are you more preoccupied with other people or things?

20 _____ _____

_____

_____

_____

20 _____ _____

_____

_____

_____

20 _____ _____

_____

_____

_____

20 _____ _____

_____

_____

_____

20 _____ _____

_____

_____

_____

February

... cease to do evil, learn to do good; seek justice, correct oppression; bring justice to the fatherless, plead the widow's cause.
—Isaiah 1:16b–17 (ESV)

How are you seeking justice and correcting oppression?

20 _____ _____

_____

_____

_____

20 _____ _____

_____

_____

_____

20 _____ _____

_____

_____

_____

20 _____ _____

_____

_____

_____

20 _____ _____

_____

_____

_____

February

17

A false balance is an abomination to the Lord, but a just weight is his delight. —Proverbs 11:1 (ESV)

Have you been dishonest about anything lately?

20 _____ _____

_____

_____

_____

20 _____ _____

_____

_____

_____

20 _____ _____

_____

_____

_____

20 _____ _____

_____

_____

_____

20 _____ _____

_____

_____

_____

February

And he withdrew himself into the wilderness, and prayed. —Luke 5:16 (KJV)

What's one way you might better prioritize time alone with God?

20 ___ _____

_____

_____

20 ___ _____

_____

_____

20 ___ _____

_____

_____

20 ___ _____

_____

_____

20 ___ _____

_____

_____

February

19

Cast thy burden upon the Lord, and he shall sustain thee: he shall never suffer the righteous to be moved. —Psalm 55:22 (KJV)

What burdens do you need to cast upon the Lord?

20 _____ _____

_____

_____

_____

20 _____ _____

_____

_____

_____

20 _____ _____

_____

_____

_____

20 _____ _____

_____

_____

_____

20 _____ _____

_____

_____

_____

February

Thou wilt keep him in perfect peace, whose mind is stayed on thee: because he trusteth in thee. —Isaiah 26:3 (KJV)

Are you experiencing "perfect peace"? What does it mean to have your mind stayed on God?

20 _____ _____

_____

_____

_____

20 _____ _____

_____

_____

_____

20 _____ _____

_____

_____

_____

20 _____ _____

_____

_____

_____

20 _____ _____

_____

_____

_____

February

O give thanks unto the Lord; for he is good: because his mercy endureth for ever. —Psalm 118:1 (KJV)

How are you experiencing God's goodness and mercy?

20 _____ _____

_____

_____

20 _____ _____

_____

_____

20 _____ _____

_____

_____

20 _____ _____

_____

_____

20 _____ _____

_____

_____

February

Purge me with hyssop, and I shall be clean: wash me, and I shall be whiter than snow. —Psalm 51:7 (KJV)

Are you hanging on to any guilt? What does the psalmist tell you about that?

20 _____ _____

_____

_____

20 _____ _____

_____

_____

20 _____ _____

_____

_____

20 _____ _____

_____

_____

20 _____ _____

_____

_____

_____

February

23

The LORD is on my side; I will not fear: what can man do unto me?
—Psalm 118:6 (KJV)

How might your perspective or current experiences shift if you focused on walking with God rather than what people think or feel about you?

20 _____ _____

_____

_____

_____

20 _____ _____

_____

_____

_____

20 _____ _____

_____

_____

_____

20 _____ _____

_____

_____

_____

20 _____ _____

_____

_____

_____

February

24

O Lord, open thou my lips; and my mouth shall shew forth thy praise. —Psalm 51:15 (KJV)

Write a brief prayer asking God to make Himself known to you, so that even in the midst of struggle, your first response is to praise Him for who He is.

20 _____ _____

_____

_____

20 _____ _____

_____

_____

20 _____ _____

_____

_____

20 _____ _____

_____

_____

20 _____ _____

_____

_____

25

February

It is better to trust in the Lord than to put confidence in man.
—Psalm 118:8 (KJV)

When has putting confidence in a person been disappointing?
Do you feel like you can trust God with all of yourself, your
relationships, your work, your past?

20 _____ _____

_____

_____

20 _____ _____

_____

_____

20 _____ _____

_____

_____

20 _____ _____

_____

_____

20 _____ _____

_____

_____

February

26

As one whom his mother comforteth, so will I comfort you . . .
—*Isaiah 66:13 (KJV)*

How have you experienced God's comfort in the past? Where do you need to experience it today?

20 _____

_____

_____

_____

20 _____

_____

_____

_____

20 _____

_____

_____

_____

20 _____

_____

_____

_____

20 _____

_____

_____

_____

February

Do all things without murmurings and disputings: That ye may be blameless and harmless, the sons of God, without rebuke, in the midst of a crooked and perverse nation, among whom ye shine as lights in the world . . . —Philippians 2:14–15 (KJV)

How are you shining as a light in the world?

20 _____

_____

_____

20 _____

_____

_____

20 _____

_____

_____

20 _____

_____

_____

20 _____

_____

_____

February

Finally, brethren, whatsoever things are true, whatsoever things are honest, whatsoever things are just, whatsoever things are pure, whatsoever things are lovely, whatsoever things are of good report; if there be any virtue, and if there be any praise, think on these things. —Philippians 4:8 (KJV)

List some praiseworthy things.

20 _____ _____

_____

_____

20 _____ _____

_____

_____

20 _____ _____

_____

_____

20 _____ _____

_____

_____

20 _____ _____

_____

_____

March

1

Now the God of patience and consolation grant you to be likeminded one toward another according to Christ Jesus . . .
—Romans 15:5 (KJV)

Are you handling disagreements with other believers through God's patience and endurance, or are you trying to settle matters in your own way?

20 _____ _____

_____

_____

_____

20 _____ _____

_____

_____

_____

20 _____ _____

_____

_____

_____

20 _____ _____

_____

_____

_____

20 _____ _____

_____

_____

_____

March

And let us not be weary in well doing: for in due season we shall reap, if we faint not. —Galatians 6:9 (KJV)

How will you bless someone today?

20 _____ _____

_____

_____

_____

20 _____ _____

_____

_____

_____

20 _____ _____

_____

_____

_____

20 _____ _____

_____

_____

_____

20 _____ _____

_____

_____

_____

March

3

Thou wilt shew me the path of life: in thy presence is fulness of joy; at thy right hand there are pleasures for evermore. —Psalm 16:11 (KJV)

Are there lesser life pleasures that are keeping you from the fullness of joy in Jesus?

20 _____ _____

_____

_____

20 _____ _____

_____

_____

20 _____ _____

_____

_____

20 _____ _____

_____

_____

20 _____ _____

_____

_____

March

4

I can do all things through Christ which strengtheneth me.
—Philippians 4:13 (KJV)

What are you tempted to feel like you can't do?

20 _____ _____

_____

_____

20 _____ _____

_____

_____

20 _____ _____

_____

_____

20 _____ _____

_____

_____

20 _____ _____

_____

_____

_____

March

5

[Love] does not dishonor others, it is not self-seeking, it is not easily angered, it keeps no record of wrongs. —*1 Corinthians 13:5 (NIV)*

Based on this verse, are you really loving the people you say you love? Write a brief prayer asking God to change your heart in whatever way yours needs changing.

20 _____ _____

_____

_____

20 _____ _____

_____

_____

20 _____ _____

_____

_____

20 _____ _____

_____

_____

20 _____ _____

_____

_____

March

Trust in him at all times; ye people, pour out your heart before him: God is a refuge for us. Selah. —Psalm 62:8 (KJV)

In what area is it hard to trust God right now?

20 _____ _____

_____

_____

20 _____ _____

_____

_____

20 _____ _____

_____

_____

20 _____ _____

_____

_____

20 _____ _____

_____

_____

March

*Fear not: for I have redeemed thee, I have called thee by thy name;
thou art mine. —Isaiah 43:1b (KJV)*

Does remembering that you are God's beloved and chosen son
or daughter change anything for you right now?

20 ___ _____

_____

_____

20 ___ _____

_____

_____

_____

20 ___ _____

_____

_____

_____

20 ___ _____

_____

_____

_____

20 ___ _____

_____

_____

_____

And why take ye thought for raiment? Consider the lilies of the field, how they grow; they toil not, neither do they spin: And yet I say unto you, That even Solomon in all his glory was not arrayed like one of these. —Matthew 6:28–29 (KJV)

How has God provided for you recently?

20 _____ _____

_____

_____

20 _____ _____

_____

_____

20 _____ _____

_____

_____

20 _____ _____

_____

_____

20 _____ _____

_____

_____

_____

March

And Jesus answered and said unto her, Martha, Martha, thou art careful and troubled about many things: But one thing is needful: and Mary hath chosen that good part, which shall not be taken away from her. —Luke 10:41–42 (KJV)

Are there priorities you need to take down a notch in order to put time with Jesus first?

20 _____ _____

_____

_____

_____

20 _____ _____

_____

_____

_____

20 _____ _____

_____

_____

_____

20 _____ _____

_____

_____

_____

20 _____ _____

_____

_____

_____

March

Return unto thy rest, O my soul; for the LORD hath dealt bountifully with thee. —Psalm 116:7 (KJV)

How has God dealt bountifully with your soul?

20 _____ _____

_____

_____

_____

20 _____ _____

_____

_____

_____

20 _____ _____

_____

_____

_____

20 _____ _____

_____

_____

_____

20 _____ _____

_____

_____

_____

March

11

But rather seek ye the kingdom of God; and all these things shall be added unto you. —Luke 12:31 (KJV)

How are you seeking the kingdom of God?

20 _____ _____

_____

_____

20 _____ _____

_____

_____

20 _____ _____

_____

_____

20 _____ _____

_____

_____

20 _____ _____

_____

_____

March

Thou art all fair, my love; there is no spot in thee. —Song of Solomon 4:7 (KJV)

What does it feel like to know this is how God sees you?

20 _____ _____

_____

_____

20 _____ _____

_____

_____

20 _____ _____

_____

_____

20 _____ _____

_____

_____

20 _____ _____

_____

_____

_____

March

In the day that I called, you answered me. You encouraged me with strength in my soul. —Psalm 138:3 (WEB)

How do you need God's help today?

20 _____ _____

_____

_____

20 _____ _____

_____

_____

20 _____ _____

_____

_____

20 _____ _____

_____

_____

_____

20 _____ _____

_____

_____

_____

March

14

Now unto him that is able to do exceeding abundantly above all that we ask or think, according to the power that worketh in us . . .
—Ephesians 3:20 (KJV)

Are there things you're afraid to ask God for, or even to think about wanting?

20 _____ _____

_____

_____

20 _____ _____

_____

_____

20 _____ _____

_____

_____

20 _____ _____

_____

_____

20 _____ _____

_____

_____

March

There is therefore now no condemnation to them which are in Christ Jesus, who walk not after the flesh, but after the Spirit.
—Romans 8:1 (KJV)

Do you feel condemned? How does this verse speak to that feeling?

20 _____ _____

_____

_____

_____

20 _____ _____

_____

_____

_____

20 _____ _____

_____

_____

_____

20 _____ _____

_____

_____

_____

20 _____ _____

_____

_____

_____

March

For the LORD taketh pleasure in his people: he will beautify the meek with salvation. —Psalm 149:4 (KJV)

Meekness is not often praised in our world today, but there is a good and right kind of meekness that comes through the security of knowing God takes pleasure in you and the humility of knowing you need His saving grace. Where might meekness be lacking in your life?

20 _____ _____

_____

_____

20 _____ _____

_____

_____

20 _____ _____

_____

_____

20 _____ _____

_____

_____

20 _____ _____

_____

_____

March

But may the God of all grace, who called you to his eternal glory by Christ Jesus, after you have suffered a little while, perfect, establish, strengthen, and settle you. —1 Peter 5:10 (WEB)

How has God used suffering to shape you in good ways?

20 _____ _____

_____

_____

20 _____ _____

_____

_____

20 _____ _____

_____

_____

20 _____ _____

_____

_____

20 _____ _____

_____

_____

18

The LORD is nigh unto them that are of a broken heart; and saveth such as be of a contrite spirit. —Psalm 34:18 (KJV)

How is your heart hurting?

20 _____ _____

_____

_____

_____

20 _____ _____

_____

_____

_____

20 _____ _____

_____

_____

_____

20 _____ _____

_____

_____

_____

20 _____ _____

_____

_____

_____

March

19

. . . the joy of the Lord is your strength. —*Nehemiah 8:10 (KJV)*

How would you describe the joy of the Lord in your life right now?

20 _____ _____

_____

_____

20 _____ _____

_____

_____

20 _____ _____

_____

_____

20 _____ _____

_____

_____

20 _____ _____

_____

_____

_____

March

. . . for your heavenly Father knoweth that ye have need of all these things. But seek ye first the kingdom of God, and his righteousness; and all these things shall be added unto you. —Matthew 6:32–33 (KJV)

What might you be seeking more than the kingdom of God?

20 _____ _____

_____

_____

_____

20 _____ _____

_____

_____

_____

20 _____ _____

_____

_____

_____

20 _____ _____

_____

_____

_____

20 _____ _____

_____

_____

_____

21

But my God shall supply all your need according to his riches in glory by Christ Jesus. —Philippians 4:19 (KJV)

What are your needs right now?

20 _____ _____

_____

_____

_____

20 _____ _____

_____

_____

_____

20 _____ _____

_____

_____

_____

20 _____ _____

_____

_____

_____

20 _____ _____

_____

_____

_____

March

Wherefore, my beloved brethren, let every man be swift to hear, slow to speak, slow to wrath . . . —James 1:19 (KJV)

Who in your life do you need to spend more time listening to?

20 _____ _____

_____

_____

_____

20 _____ _____

_____

_____

_____

20 _____ _____

_____

_____

_____

20 _____ _____

_____

_____

_____

20 _____ _____

_____

_____

_____

March

He that spared not his own Son, but delivered him up for us all, how shall he not with him also freely give us all things? —Romans 8:32 (KJV)

Do you feel like God is generous with you personally? Why or why not?

20 _____ _____

_____

_____

20 _____ _____

_____

_____

20 _____ _____

_____

_____

20 _____ _____

_____

_____

_____

20 _____ _____

_____

_____

_____

March

24

Shew me thy ways, O Lord; teach me thy paths. —Psalm 25:4 (KJV)

Are you seeking direction for something specific?

20 _____ _____

_____

_____

20 _____ _____

_____

_____

20 _____ _____

_____

_____

20 _____ _____

_____

_____

20 _____ _____

_____

_____

March

25

. . . your Father knoweth what things ye have need of, before ye ask him. —*Matthew 6:8b (KJV)*

Is there anything you're afraid to ask God for? Why?

20 _____ _____

_____

_____

20 _____ _____

_____

_____

20 _____ _____

_____

_____

20 _____ _____

_____

_____

20 _____ _____

_____

_____

March

26

. . . for I have learned, in whatsoever state I am, therewith to be content. —Philippians 4:11 (KJV)

In what ways are you experiencing contentment or discontentment?

20 _____ _____

_____

_____

_____

20 _____ _____

_____

_____

_____

20 _____ _____

_____

_____

_____

20 _____ _____

_____

_____

_____

20 _____ _____

_____

_____

_____

March

Even to old age I am he, and even to gray hairs I will carry you. I have made, and I will bear. Yes, I will carry, and will deliver. —Isaiah 46:4 (WEB)

How do you need to be carried or delivered right now?

20 _____ _____

_____

_____

20 _____ _____

_____

_____

20 _____ _____

_____

_____

20 _____ _____

_____

_____

_____

20 _____ _____

_____

_____

_____

March

28

O Lord, how manifold are thy works! in wisdom hast thou made them all: the earth is full of thy riches. —Psalm 104:24 (KJV)

Write your own brief psalm of praise.

20 _____ _____

_____

_____

_____

20 _____ _____

_____

_____

_____

20 _____ _____

_____

_____

_____

20 _____ _____

_____

_____

_____

20 _____ _____

_____

_____

_____

March

I will praise thee, O LORD, with my whole heart; I will shew forth all thy marvellous works. —Psalm 9:1 (KJV)

Does praising God feel easy or like something you have to practice?

20 _____ _____

_____

_____

20 _____ _____

_____

_____

20 _____ _____

_____

_____

20 _____ _____

_____

_____

20 _____ _____

_____

_____

March

But mine eyes are unto thee, O GOD the Lord: in thee is my trust; leave not my soul destitute. —Psalm 141:8 (KJV)

Are you looking to God for help, or are there other things you're trusting in more than God?

20 _____ _____

_____

_____

_____

20 _____ _____

_____

_____

_____

20 _____ _____

_____

_____

_____

20 _____ _____

_____

_____

_____

20 _____ _____

_____

_____

_____

March

31

Let us therefore come boldly unto the throne of grace, that we may obtain mercy, and find grace to help in time of need. —Hebrews 4:16 (KJV)

Which lost friends are you boldly asking God to rescue?

20 _____ _____

_____

_____

_____

20 _____ _____

_____

_____

_____

20 _____ _____

_____

_____

_____

20 _____ _____

_____

_____

_____

20 _____ _____

_____

_____

_____

April

For we are his workmanship, created in Christ Jesus unto good works, which God hath before ordained that we should walk in them. —Ephesians 2:10 (KJV)

Reflect on what it means to be God's workmanship.

20 ___ _____

_____

_____

20 ___ _____

_____

_____

20 ___ _____

_____

_____

20 ___ _____

_____

_____

20 ___ _____

_____

_____

April

Thou art worthy, O Lord, to receive glory and honour and power: for thou hast created all things, and for thy pleasure they are and were created. —Revelation 4:11 (KJV)

Reflect on the truth that you, as God's creation, give Him pleasure.

20 _____ _____

_____

_____

_____

20 _____ _____

_____

_____

_____

20 _____ _____

_____

_____

_____

20 _____ _____

_____

_____

_____

20 _____ _____

_____

_____

_____

April

3

For I have satiated the weary soul, and I have replenished every sorrowful soul. —Jeremiah 31:25 (KJV)

How are you allowing God to satisfy and replenish your soul?

20 _____ _____

_____

_____

20 _____ _____

_____

_____

20 _____ _____

_____

_____

20 _____ _____

_____

_____

20 _____ _____

_____

_____

4

April

Every good gift and every perfect gift is from above, and cometh down from the Father of lights, with whom is no variableness, neither shadow of turning. —James 1:17 (KJV)

What are some good gifts in your life?

20 _____ _____

_____

_____

20 _____ _____

_____

_____

20 _____ _____

_____

_____

20 _____ _____

_____

_____

20 _____ _____

_____

_____

April

5

Blessed are they that mourn: for they shall be comforted.
—Matthew 5:4 (KJV)

How have you experienced God's comfort?

20 _____ _____

_____

_____

20 _____ _____

_____

_____

20 _____ _____

_____

_____

20 _____ _____

_____

_____

20 _____ _____

_____

_____

April

6

To do justice and judgment is more acceptable to the LORD than sacrifice. —Proverbs 21:3 (KJV)

How are you working toward justice?

20 ___ _____

_____

_____

20 ___ _____

_____

_____

20 ___ _____

_____

_____

20 ___ _____

_____

_____

20 ___ _____

_____

_____

April

Thou hast turned for me my mourning into dancing: thou hast put off my sackcloth, and girded me with gladness . . . —Psalm 30:11 (KJV)

How has God transformed heartache into joy in your life?

20 _____ _____

_____

_____

20 _____ _____

_____

_____

20 _____ _____

_____

_____

20 _____ _____

_____

_____

20 _____ _____

_____

_____

April

"But I tell you, love your enemies, bless those who curse you, do good to those who hate you, and pray for those who mistreat you and persecute you . . ." —Matthew 5:44 (WEB)

How are you blessing your enemies?

20 _____ _____

_____

_____

_____

20 _____ _____

_____

_____

_____

20 _____ _____

_____

_____

_____

20 _____ _____

_____

_____

_____

20 _____ _____

_____

_____

_____

April

Thou openest thine hand, and satisfiest the desire of every living thing. —Psalm 145:16 (KJV)

What godly desires do you have?

20 _____ _____

_____

_____

20 _____ _____

_____

_____

20 _____ _____

_____

_____

20 _____ _____

_____

_____

20 _____ _____

_____

_____

April

"But when you do merciful deeds, don't let your left hand know what your right hand does, so that your merciful deeds may be in secret, then your Father who sees in secret will reward you openly."
—Matthew 6:3–4 (WEB)

What is motivating the generous things you do?

20 _____ _____

_____

_____

_____

20 _____ _____

_____

_____

_____

20 _____ _____

_____

_____

_____

20 _____ _____

_____

_____

_____

20 _____ _____

_____

_____

_____

April

11

My voice shalt thou hear in the morning, O Lord; in the morning will I direct my prayer unto thee, and will look up. —Psalm 5:3 (KJV)

Write a brief prayer about anything that's on your heart.

20 _____ _____

_____

_____

_____

20 _____ _____

_____

_____

_____

20 _____ _____

_____

_____

_____

20 _____ _____

_____

_____

_____

20 _____ _____

_____

_____

_____

April

"For everyone who asks receives. He who seeks finds. To him who knocks it will be opened." —Matthew 7:8 (WEB)

Do you believe this? Why or why not?

20 _____ _____

_____

_____

20 _____ _____

_____

_____

20 _____ _____

_____

_____

20 _____ _____

_____

_____

20 _____ _____

_____

_____

April

For he satisfieth the longing soul, and filleth the hungry soul with goodness. —Psalm 107:9 (KJV)

What are your deepest longings?

20 _____ _____

_____

_____

20 _____ _____

_____

_____

20 _____ _____

_____

_____

20 _____ _____

_____

_____

20 _____ _____

_____

_____

_____

April

14

Keep thy heart with all diligence; for out of it are the issues of life.
—Proverbs 4:23 (KJV)

Is there a situation where you're blaming another person without looking diligently at your own heart?

20 _____ _____

_____

_____

_____

20 _____ _____

_____

_____

_____

20 _____ _____

_____

_____

_____

20 _____ _____

_____

_____

_____

20 _____ _____

_____

_____

_____

April

15

"Take my yoke upon you and learn from me, for I am gentle and humble in heart; and you will find rest for your souls." —Matthew 11:29 (WEB)

Meditate on Jesus being gentle and humble and write down any insights you have.

20 _____ _____

_____

_____

_____

20 _____ _____

_____

_____

_____

20 _____ _____

_____

_____

_____

20 _____ _____

_____

_____

_____

20 _____ _____

_____

_____

_____

April

16

Stand fast therefore in the liberty wherewith Christ hath made us free, and be not entangled again with the yoke of bondage.
—Galatians 5:1 (KJV)

Is anything or anyone (including yourself) claiming to have more truth or power in your life than Christ's redeeming blood?

20 _____ _____

_____

_____

_____

20 _____ _____

_____

_____

_____

20 _____ _____

_____

_____

_____

20 _____ _____

_____

_____

_____

20 _____ _____

_____

_____

_____

April

17

Bless the Lord, O my soul, and forget not all his benefits: Who forgiveth all thine iniquities; who healeth all thy diseases; Who redeemeth thy life from destruction; who crowneth thee with lovingkindness and tender mercies . . . —Psalm 103:2–4 (KJV)

List some things God has done or is doing in your life.

20 _____ _____

_____

_____

20 _____ _____

_____

_____

20 _____ _____

_____

_____

20 _____ _____

_____

_____

20 _____ _____

_____

_____

April

My soul waiteth for the Lord more than they that watch for the morning: I say, more than they that watch for the morning.
—Psalm 130:6 (KJV)

What does waiting for the Lord mean? What does it look like in your life?

20 ____ _____

_____

_____

_____

20 ____ _____

_____

_____

_____

20 ____ _____

_____

_____

_____

20 ____ _____

_____

_____

_____

20 ____ _____

_____

_____

_____

19

April

Submit yourselves therefore to God. Resist the devil, and he will flee from you. —James 4:7 (KJV)

Are you resisting submission to God in any area, big or small? Who can you ask to pray with you and keep you accountable?

20 _____ _____

_____

_____

_____

20 _____ _____

_____

_____

_____

20 _____ _____

_____

_____

_____

20 _____ _____

_____

_____

_____

20 _____ _____

_____

_____

_____

April

20

Mine eyes are ever toward the LORD; for he shall pluck my feet out of the net. —Psalm 25:15 (KJV)

What circumstances or relationships are threatening to steal your gaze?

20 _____ _____

_____

_____

_____

20 _____ _____

_____

_____

_____

20 _____ _____

_____

_____

_____

20 _____ _____

_____

_____

_____

20 _____ _____

_____

_____

_____

April

He restores my soul. He leads me in paths of righteousness for his name's sake. —Psalm 23:3 (ESV)

How has God restored your soul?

20 _____ _____

_____

_____

20 _____ _____

_____

_____

_____

20 _____ _____

_____

_____

_____

20 _____ _____

_____

_____

_____

20 _____ _____

_____

_____

_____

April

Draw nigh to God, and he will draw nigh to you. Cleanse your hands, ye sinners; and purify your hearts, ye double minded.
—James 4:8 (KJV)

Ask God to search your heart and mind for any hidden filth. Write a prayer or jot down what He revealed.

20 ____ _____

_____

_____

20 ____ _____

_____

_____

20 ____ _____

_____

_____

20 ____ _____

_____

_____

20 ____ _____

_____

_____

April

23

My help cometh from the LORD, which made heaven and earth.
—Psalm 121:2 (KJV)

What are some ways God has revealed His power to you, either through the Bible or in your life specifically?

20 _____ _____

_____

_____

20 _____ _____

_____

_____

20 _____ _____

_____

_____

20 _____ _____

_____

_____

20 _____ _____

_____

_____

April

24

For because he himself has suffered when tempted, he is able to help those who are being tempted. —Hebrews 2:18 (ESV)

What temptations are you facing? How are you fighting them?

20 _____ _____

_____

_____

20 _____ _____

_____

_____

20 _____ _____

_____

_____

20 _____ _____

_____

_____

20 _____ _____

_____

_____

April

25

O satisfy us early with thy mercy; that we may rejoice and be glad all our days. —Psalm 90:14 (KJV)

In what (or in whom) are you seeking satisfaction?

20 _____ _____

_____

_____

20 _____ _____

_____

_____

20 _____ _____

_____

_____

20 _____ _____

_____

_____

20 _____ _____

_____

_____

26

April

....

Behold, happy is the man whom God correcteth: therefore despise not thou the chastening of the Almighty. —Job 5:17 (KJV)

How is God correcting you?

20 _____ _____

_____

_____

20 _____ _____

_____

_____

20 _____ _____

_____

_____

20 _____ _____

_____

_____

20 _____ _____

_____

_____

April

27

. . . for he that loveth another hath fulfilled the law. —Romans 13:8b (KJV)

In what ways are you living out God's love?

20 _____ _____

_____

_____

20 _____ _____

_____

_____

20 _____ _____

_____

_____

20 _____ _____

_____

_____

20 _____ _____

_____

_____

April

Deliver me out of the mire, and let me not sink: let me be delivered from them that hate me, and out of the deep waters. —Psalm 69:14 (KJV)

Write your own plea to God. Don't hold back the biggest feelings or deepest needs.

20 _____ _____

_____

_____

_____

20 _____ _____

_____

_____

_____

20 _____ _____

_____

_____

_____

20 _____ _____

_____

_____

_____

20 _____ _____

_____

_____

_____

April

29

And the Lord shall help them, and deliver them: he shall deliver them from the wicked, and save them, because they trust in him.
—Psalm 37:40 (KJV)

In what ways do you need to trust God right now?

20 _____ _____

_____

_____

20 _____ _____

_____

_____

20 _____ _____

_____

_____

20 _____ _____

_____

_____

20 _____ _____

_____

_____

April

30

He only is my rock and my salvation: he is my defence; I shall not be moved. —Psalm 62:6 (KJV)

Are you seeking a sense of security from anything other than God?

20 _____ _____

_____

_____

_____

20 _____ _____

_____

_____

_____

20 _____ _____

_____

_____

_____

20 _____ _____

_____

_____

_____

20 _____ _____

_____

_____

_____

May

And the Lord shall guide thee continually, and satisfy thy soul in drought, and make fat thy bones: and thou shalt be like a watered garden, and like a spring of water, whose waters fail not. —Isaiah 58:11 (KJV)

How does this promise apply to your life right now?

20 _____ _____

_____

_____

20 _____ _____

_____

_____

20 _____ _____

_____

_____

20 _____ _____

_____

_____

20 _____ _____

_____

_____

May

Who is a God like unto thee, that pardoneth iniquity, and passeth by the transgression of the remnant of his heritage? he retaineth not his anger for ever, because he delighteth in mercy. —Micah 7:18 (KJV)

God delights in mercy. Do you? What might that look like in your life?

20 _____ _____

_____

_____

20 _____ _____

_____

_____

20 _____ _____

_____

_____

20 _____ _____

_____

_____

20 _____ _____

_____

_____

May

Hatred stirs up strife, but love covers all offenses. —Proverbs 10:12 (ESV)

Are you holding any grudges? How can you start to let go of them?

20 _____ _____

_____

_____

_____

20 _____ _____

_____

_____

_____

20 _____ _____

_____

_____

_____

20 _____ _____

_____

_____

_____

20 _____ _____

_____

_____

_____

4

May

As far as the east is from the west, so far hath he removed our transgressions from us. —Psalm 103:12 (KJV)

Write a brief prayer of praise to God for His forgiveness.

20 _____ _____

_____

_____

_____

20 _____ _____

_____

_____

_____

20 _____ _____

_____

_____

_____

20 _____ _____

_____

_____

_____

20 _____ _____

_____

_____

_____

May

And whatsoever ye do in word or deed, do all in the name of the Lord Jesus, giving thanks to God and the Father by him.
—Colossians 3:17 (KJV)

Is there any part of your life in which you're seeking glory for yourself rather than for Jesus?

20 _____ _____

_____

_____

20 _____ _____

_____

_____

20 _____ _____

_____

_____

20 _____ _____

_____

_____

20 _____ _____

_____

_____

_____

6

May

A soft answer turns away wrath, but a harsh word stirs up anger.
—*Proverbs 15:1*

Reflect on a time you experienced giving or receiving a soft answer or a harsh word.

20 _____ _____

_____

_____

_____

20 _____ _____

_____

_____

_____

20 _____ _____

_____

_____

_____

20 _____ _____

_____

_____

_____

20 _____ _____

_____

_____

_____

May

For I acknowledge my transgressions: and my sin is ever before me
—Psalm 51:3 (KJV)

Reflect on some of the sins you need to repent of.

20 _____ _____

_____

_____

20 _____ _____

_____

_____

20 _____ _____

_____

_____

20 _____ _____

_____

_____

_____

20 _____ _____

_____

_____

_____

May

The hand of the diligent will rule, while the slothful will be put to forced labor. —Proverbs 12:24 (ESV)

In what ways have you been diligent or slothful lately?

20 _____ _____

_____

_____

_____

20 _____ _____

_____

_____

_____

20 _____ _____

_____

_____

_____

20 _____ _____

_____

_____

_____

20 _____ _____

_____

_____

_____

May

[Love] beareth all things, believeth all things, hopeth all things, endureth all things. —1 Corinthians 13:7 (KJV)

Write a prayer asking God to give you love to handle whatever tough relationship or situation you're in.

20 _____ _____

_____

_____

_____

20 _____ _____

_____

_____

_____

20 _____ _____

_____

_____

_____

20 _____ _____

_____

_____

_____

20 _____ _____

_____

_____

_____

May

10

*And if children, then heirs; heirs of God, and joint-heirs with Christ;
if so be that we suffer with him, that we may be also glorified
together.* —Romans 8:17 (KJV)

What does it mean to be a joint-heir with Christ?

20 _____ _____

_____

_____

_____

20 _____ _____

_____

_____

_____

20 _____ _____

_____

_____

_____

20 _____ _____

_____

_____

_____

20 _____ _____

_____

_____

_____

May

And he said unto her, Daughter, be of good comfort: thy faith hath made thee whole; go in peace. —Luke 8:48 (KJV)

In what way do you need comfort, healing, or peace? How might faith play a role in receiving that?

20 _____ _____

_____

_____

20 _____ _____

_____

_____

20 _____ _____

_____

_____

20 _____ _____

_____

_____

20 _____ _____

_____

_____

_____

12

May

Create in me a clean heart, O God; and renew a right spirit within me. —Psalm 51:10 (KJV)

In what ways do you need cleansing or renewal?

20 _____ _____

_____

_____

_____

20 _____ _____

_____

_____

_____

20 _____ _____

_____

_____

_____

20 _____ _____

_____

_____

_____

20 _____ _____

_____

_____

_____

May

For ye have not received the spirit of bondage again to fear; but ye have received the Spirit of adoption, whereby we cry, Abba, Father.
—Romans 8:15 (KJV)

How does this verse speak to you today?

20 _____ _____

_____

_____

20 _____ _____

_____

_____

20 _____ _____

_____

_____

20 _____ _____

_____

_____

20 _____ _____

_____

_____

May

And be not conformed to this world: but be ye transformed by the renewing of your mind, that ye may prove what is that good, and acceptable, and perfect, will of God. —Romans 12:2 (KJV)

How are you being conformed or transformed?

20 _____ _____

_____

_____

_____

20 _____ _____

_____

_____

_____

20 _____ _____

_____

_____

_____

20 _____ _____

_____

_____

_____

20 _____ _____

_____

_____

_____

15

May

And above all these things put on charity, which is the bond of perfectness. —Colossians 3:14 (KJV)

How is God loving others through you?

20 _____ _____

_____

_____

_____

20 _____ _____

_____

_____

_____

20 _____ _____

_____

_____

_____

20 _____ _____

_____

_____

_____

20 _____ _____

_____

_____

_____

May

For the Lord is good; his mercy is everlasting; and his truth endureth to all generations. —Psalm 100:5 (KJV)

List some ways that God is good, merciful, or true.

20 _____ _____

_____

_____

_____

20 _____ _____

_____

_____

_____

20 _____ _____

_____

_____

_____

20 _____ _____

_____

_____

_____

20 _____ _____

_____

_____

_____

May

17

The Spirit itself beareth witness with our spirit, that we are the children of God . . . —Romans 8:16 (KJV)

What does it mean to be a child of God?

20 _____ _____

_____

_____

20 _____ _____

_____

_____

20 _____ _____

_____

_____

20 _____ _____

_____

_____

20 _____ _____

_____

_____

May

18

How excellent is thy lovingkindness, O God! therefore the children of men put their trust under the shadow of thy wings. —Psalm 36:7 (KJV)

How has God protected or provided for you?

20 _____ _____

_____

_____

_____

20 _____ _____

_____

_____

_____

20 _____ _____

_____

_____

_____

20 _____ _____

_____

_____

_____

20 _____ _____

_____

_____

_____

May

The LORD hath appeared of old unto me, saying, Yea, I have loved thee with an everlasting love: therefore with lovingkindness have I drawn thee. —Jeremiah 31:3 (KJV)

What does God's love look like in your life right now?

20 _____ _____

_____

_____

_____

20 _____ _____

_____

_____

_____

20 _____ _____

_____

_____

_____

20 _____ _____

_____

_____

_____

20 _____ _____

_____

_____

_____

May

That Christ may dwell in your hearts by faith; that ye, being rooted and grounded in love, May be able to comprehend with all saints what is the breadth, and length, and depth, and height; And to know the love of Christ, which passeth knowledge, that ye might be filled with all the fulness of God. —Ephesians 3:17–19 (KJV)

How has God shown His love in the Bible? How has He shown His love to you personally?

20 _____ _____

_____

_____

_____

20 _____ _____

_____

_____

_____

20 _____ _____

_____

_____

_____

20 _____ _____

_____

_____

_____

20 _____ _____

_____

_____

_____

21

May

For whom the Lord loveth he correcteth; even as a father the son in whom he delighteth. —Proverbs 3:12 (KJV)

What kind of godly correction have you experienced lately?

20 _____ _____

_____

_____

20 _____ _____

_____

_____

20 _____ _____

_____

_____

20 _____ _____

_____

_____

20 _____ _____

_____

_____

_____

May

. . . The beloved of the Lord shall dwell in safety by him; and the Lord shall cover him all the day long, and he shall dwell between his shoulders. —Deuteronomy 33:12 (KJV)

List a few of your fears or anxieties. How does this verse apply to them?

20 _____ _____

_____

_____

20 _____ _____

_____

_____

20 _____ _____

_____

_____

20 _____ _____

_____

_____

20 _____ _____

_____

_____

23

May

Say not thou, What is the cause that the former days were better than these? for thou dost not enquire wisely concerning this.
—Ecclesiastes 7:10 (KJV)

In what ways might you be stuck pining for the past?

20 _____ _____

_____

_____

20 _____ _____

_____

_____

20 _____ _____

_____

_____

20 _____ _____

_____

_____

20 _____ _____

_____

_____

24

May

Thou hast also given me the shield of thy salvation: and thy right hand hath holden me up, and thy gentleness hath made me great.
—Psalm 18:35 (KJV)

What challenge can you face knowing you have God's shield, God's right hand, and God's gentleness making you great?

20 _____ _____

_____

_____

_____

20 _____ _____

_____

_____

_____

20 _____ _____

_____

_____

_____

20 _____ _____

_____

_____

_____

20 _____ _____

_____

_____

_____

May

25

The eyes of the LORD are upon the righteous, and his ears are open unto their cry. —Psalm 34:15 (KJV)

Is there any prayer you're holding back because you don't really, fully, totally believe God sees you and hears you and wants what's best for you?

20 _____ _____

_____

_____

_____

20 _____ _____

_____

_____

_____

20 _____ _____

_____

_____

_____

20 _____ _____

_____

_____

_____

20 _____ _____

_____

_____

_____

26

May

Thou hast heard my voice: hide not thine ear at my breathing, at my cry. —Lamentations 3:56 (KJV)

What is weighing down your heart? Tell God about it.

20 _____ _____

_____

_____

_____

20 _____ _____

_____

_____

_____

20 _____ _____

_____

_____

_____

20 _____ _____

_____

_____

_____

20 _____ _____

_____

_____

_____

May

And the peace of God, which passeth all understanding, shall keep your hearts and minds through Christ Jesus. —Philippians 4:7 (KJV)

Describe the peace of God.

20 _____ _____

_____

_____

_____

20 _____ _____

_____

_____

_____

20 _____ _____

_____

_____

_____

20 _____ _____

_____

_____

_____

20 _____ _____

_____

_____

_____

28

May

My flesh and my heart faileth: but God is the strength of my heart, and my portion for ever. —Psalm 73:26 (KJV)

How is God strengthening you?

20 _____ _____

_____

_____

_____

20 _____ _____

_____

_____

_____

20 _____ _____

_____

_____

_____

20 _____ _____

_____

_____

_____

20 _____ _____

_____

_____

_____

May

29

I will be glad and rejoice in your loving kindness, for you have seen my affliction. You have known my soul in adversities.
—Psalm 31:7 (WEB)

We all want to be seen and known. How does it change things to remember the one true God sees and knows you more deeply than any human ever could?

20 _____ _____

_____

_____

_____

20 _____ _____

_____

_____

_____

20 _____ _____

_____

_____

_____

20 _____ _____

_____

_____

_____

20 _____ _____

_____

_____

_____

May

30

The earth is the Lord's, and the fulness thereof; the world, and they that dwell therein. —Psalm 24:1 (KJV)

How are you caring for God's earth and those who dwell on it?

20 _____ _____

_____

_____

20 _____ _____

_____

_____

20 _____ _____

_____

_____

20 _____ _____

_____

_____

_____

20 _____ _____

_____

_____

_____

May

I waited patiently for the Lord; and he inclined unto me, and heard my cry. —Psalm 40:1 (KJV)

Write down your cry to God.

20 _____ _____

_____

_____

_____

20 _____ _____

_____

_____

_____

20 _____ _____

_____

_____

_____

20 _____ _____

_____

_____

_____

20 _____ _____

_____

_____

_____

June

The meek will he guide in judgment: and the meek will he teach his way. —Psalm 25:9 (KJV)

What are some examples of meekness in the Bible or in the lives of Christians you know or have read about?

20 _____ _____

_____

_____

20 _____ _____

_____

_____

20 _____ _____

_____

_____

20 _____ _____

_____

_____

_____

20 _____ _____

_____

_____

_____

2

June

I will be glad and rejoice in thee: I will sing praise to thy name, O thou most High. —Psalm 9:2 (KJV)

What are you grateful for?

20 _____ _____

_____

_____

_____

20 _____ _____

_____

_____

_____

20 _____ _____

_____

_____

_____

20 _____ _____

_____

_____

_____

20 _____ _____

_____

_____

_____

June

3

If we believe not, yet he abideth faithful: he cannot deny himself.
—*2 Timothy 2:13 (KJV)*

How has God been faithful, even when you have not?

20 _____ _____

_____

_____

_____

20 _____ _____

_____

_____

_____

20 _____ _____

_____

_____

_____

20 _____ _____

_____

_____

_____

20 _____ _____

_____

_____

_____

June

4

Better is a dry morsel, and quietness therewith, than an house full of sacrifices with strife. —Proverbs 17:1 (KJV)

Reflect on this verse and jot down your thoughts.

20 _____ _____

_____

_____

20 _____ _____

_____

_____

20 _____ _____

_____

_____

20 _____ _____

_____

_____

20 _____ _____

_____

_____

June

Thou compassest my path and my lying down, and art acquainted with all my ways. —Psalm 139:3 (KJV)

In what ways is it comforting, or maybe troubling instead, that God knows you inside and out?

20 _____ _____

_____

_____

_____

20 _____ _____

_____

_____

_____

20 _____ _____

_____

_____

_____

20 _____ _____

_____

_____

_____

20 _____ _____

_____

_____

_____

June

One thing have I desired of the LORD, that will I seek after; that I may dwell in the house of the LORD all the days of my life, to behold the beauty of the LORD, and to enquire in his temple. —Psalm 27:4 (KJV)

Does this verse sound like something you would write right now? Why or why not?

20 ___ _____

_____

_____

20 ___ _____

_____

_____

20 ___ _____

_____

_____

20 ___ _____

_____

_____

20 ___ _____

_____

_____

June

Be strong and of a good courage, fear not, nor be afraid of them: for the LORD thy God, he it is that doth go with thee; he will not fail thee, nor forsake thee. —Deuteronomy 31:6 (KJV)

Do you need courage and strength for any particular situation?

20 _____ _____

_____

_____

_____

20 _____ _____

_____

_____

_____

20 _____ _____

_____

_____

_____

20 _____ _____

_____

_____

_____

20 _____ _____

_____

_____

_____

June

Call unto me, and I will answer thee, and show thee great and mighty things, which thou knowest not. —Jeremiah 33:3 (KJV)

Write a short prayer asking God to reveal Himself to you however He sees fit.

20 _____ _____

_____

_____

_____

20 _____ _____

_____

_____

_____

20 _____ _____

_____

_____

_____

20 _____ _____

_____

_____

_____

20 _____ _____

_____

_____

_____

June

Be not far from me; for trouble is near; for there is none to help.
—*Psalm 22:11 (KJV)*

Describe a time you've felt helpless or alone.

20 _____ _____

_____

_____

20 _____ _____

_____

_____

20 _____ _____

_____

_____

_____

20 _____ _____

_____

_____

_____

20 _____ _____

_____

_____

_____

10

June

If ye then, being evil, know how to give good gifts unto your children, how much more shall your Father which is in heaven give good things to them that ask him? —Matthew 7:11 (KJV)

What are you asking God for today?

20 _____ _____

_____

_____

20 _____ _____

_____

_____

20 _____ _____

_____

_____

20 _____ _____

_____

_____

20 _____ _____

_____

_____

June

Thou knowest my downsitting and mine uprising, thou understandest my thought afar off. —Psalm 139:2 (KJV)

How does it feel to know God understands you?

20___ _____

_____

_____

_____

20___ _____

_____

_____

_____

20___ _____

_____

_____

_____

20___ _____

_____

_____

_____

20___ _____

_____

_____

_____

June

Ask, and it shall be given you; seek, and ye shall find; knock, and it shall be opened unto you . . . —Matthew 7:7 (KJV)

Are you stuck in any situation, habit, cycle, or problem? Write down your prayer.

20 _____ _____

_____

_____

20 _____ _____

_____

_____

20 _____ _____

_____

_____

20 _____ _____

_____

_____

_____

20 _____ _____

_____

_____

_____

June

And I will bring the blind by a way that they knew not; I will lead them in paths that they have not known: I will make darkness light before them, and crooked things straight. These things will I do unto them, and not forsake them. —Isaiah 42:16 (KJV)

What "crooked" things do you need God to make straight?

20 _____ _____

_____

_____

_____

20 _____ _____

_____

_____

_____

20 _____ _____

_____

_____

_____

20 _____ _____

_____

_____

_____

20 _____ _____

_____

_____

_____

14

June

And this is the confidence that we have in him, that, if we ask any thing according to his will, he heareth us . . . —1 John 5:14 (KJV)

What are you asking God for? Does Scripture give you reason to believe it's in His will?

20 _____ _____

_____

_____

_____

20 _____ _____

_____

_____

_____

20 _____ _____

_____

_____

_____

20 _____ _____

_____

_____

_____

20 _____ _____

_____

_____

_____

15

June

O God, be not far from me: O my God, make haste for my help.
—Psalm 71:12 (KJV)

Has asking God for help been your first instinct when trouble comes? Why or why not?

20 _____ _____

_____

_____

20 _____ _____

_____

_____

20 _____ _____

_____

_____

20 _____ _____

_____

_____

20 _____ _____

_____

_____

16

June

Charity never faileth: but whether there be prophecies, they shall fail; whether there be tongues, they shall cease; whether there be knowledge, it shall vanish away. —1 Corinthians 13:8 (KJV)

How have you experienced God's unfailing love through other people?

20 _____ _____

_____

_____

_____

20 _____ _____

_____

_____

_____

20 _____ _____

_____

_____

_____

20 _____ _____

_____

_____

_____

20 _____ _____

_____

_____

_____

June

Let your conversation be without covetousness; and be content with such things as ye have: for he hath said, I will never leave thee, nor forsake thee. —Hebrews 13:5 (KJV)

How is God's faithfulness related to contentment? In what ways do you struggle with contentment?

20 ___ _____

_____

_____

_____

20 ___ _____

_____

_____

_____

20 ___ _____

_____

_____

_____

20 ___ _____

_____

_____

_____

20 ___ _____

_____

_____

_____

June

Jesus said unto him, Thou shalt love the Lord thy God with all thy heart, and with all thy soul, and with all thy mind. —Matthew 22:37 (KJV)

What are some thoughts or feelings you have that don't align with wholehearted love for God?

20 _____ _____

_____

_____

20 _____ _____

_____

_____

_____

20 _____ _____

_____

_____

20 _____ _____

_____

_____

_____

20 _____ _____

_____

_____

_____

June

I sought the Lord, and he heard me, and delivered me from all my fears. —Psalm 34:4 (KJV)

What fears has God delivered you from?

20 _____ _____

_____

_____

20 _____ _____

_____

_____

20 _____ _____

_____

_____

20 _____ _____

_____

_____

_____

20 _____ _____

_____

_____

_____

June

Why art thou cast down, O my soul? and why art thou disquieted within me? hope thou in God: for I shall yet praise him, who is the health of my countenance, and my God. —Psalm 42:11 (KJV)

Write a few lines to your own soul. What truths does your soul need to be reminded of?

20 _____ _____

_____

_____

_____

20 _____ _____

_____

_____

_____

20 _____ _____

_____

_____

_____

20 _____ _____

_____

_____

_____

20 _____ _____

_____

_____

_____

June

Though I walk in the midst of trouble, thou wilt revive me: thou shalt stretch forth thine hand against the wrath of mine enemies, and thy right hand shall save me. —Psalm 138:7 (KJV)

What troubles are you walking through, and how is God responding?

20 _____ _____

_____

_____

20 _____ _____

_____

_____

20 _____ _____

_____

_____

20 _____ _____

_____

_____

20 _____ _____

_____

_____

June

Blessed are the merciful: for they shall obtain mercy. —Matthew 5:7 (KJV)

How could you be merciful today, or this week?

20 ____ _____

_____

_____

_____

20 ____ _____

_____

_____

_____

20 ____ _____

_____

_____

_____

20 ____ _____

_____

_____

_____

20 ____ _____

_____

_____

_____

23

June

But I am poor and sorrowful: let thy salvation, O God, set me up on high. —Psalm 69:29 (KJV)

The psalmist has no problem sharing a full range of emotions with God. What are you feeling right now?

20 _____ _____

_____

_____

20 _____ _____

_____

_____

20 _____ _____

_____

_____

20 _____ _____

_____

_____

20 _____ _____

_____

_____

June

24

"Therefore don't be anxious for tomorrow, for tomorrow will be anxious for itself. Each day's own evil is sufficient." —Matthew 6:34 (WEB)

What are you worrying about, and how do you know you can trust God with that?

20 _____ _____

_____

_____

_____

20 _____ _____

_____

_____

_____

20 _____ _____

_____

_____

_____

20 _____ _____

_____

_____

_____

20 _____ _____

_____

_____

_____

June

25

O LORD, our Lord, how excellent is thy name in all the earth! who hast set thy glory above the heavens. —Psalm 8:1 (KJV)

Write your own brief psalm of praise.

20 _____ _____

_____

_____

_____

20 _____ _____

_____

_____

_____

20 _____ _____

_____

_____

_____

20 _____ _____

_____

_____

_____

20 _____ _____

_____

_____

_____

June

Lead me in thy truth, and teach me: for thou art the God of my salvation; on thee do I wait all the day. —Psalm 25:5 (KJV)

In what ways do you need teaching or guidance right now?

20 _____ _____

_____

_____

20 _____ _____

_____

_____

20 _____ _____

_____

_____

20 _____ _____

_____

_____

_____

20 _____ _____

_____

_____

_____

June

And because ye are sons, God hath sent forth the Spirit of his Son into your hearts, crying, Abba, Father. —Galatians 4:6 (KJV)

How does it feel to remember you are a son or daughter of God, that you have every right to call God "Daddy"?

20 ___ _____

_____

_____

20 ___ _____

_____

_____

20 ___ _____

_____

_____

20 ___ _____

_____

_____

20 ___ _____

_____

_____

June

"For I know the thoughts that I think toward you," says Yahweh, "thoughts of peace, and not of evil, to give you hope and a future."
—Jeremiah 29:11 (WEB)

What good things do you believe God wants for you?

20 _____ _____

_____

_____

_____

20 _____ _____

_____

_____

_____

20 _____ _____

_____

_____

_____

20 _____ _____

_____

_____

_____

20 _____ _____

_____

_____

_____

June

The spirit of God hath made me, and the breath of the Almighty hath given me life. —Job 33:4 (KJV)

How does this verse affect how you see yourself and your life?

20 _____ _____

_____

_____

_____

20 _____ _____

_____

_____

_____

20 _____ _____

_____

_____

_____

20 _____ _____

_____

_____

_____

20 _____ _____

_____

_____

_____

June

But now, O Lord, thou art our father; we are the clay, and thou our potter; and we all are the work of thy hand. —Isaiah 64:8 (KJV)

How do you want God to shape you?

20 _____ _____

_____

_____

_____

20 _____ _____

_____

_____

_____

20 _____ _____

_____

_____

_____

20 _____ _____

_____

_____

_____

20 _____ _____

_____

_____

_____

July

But thou, when thou prayest, enter into thy closet, and when thou hast shut thy door, pray to thy Father which is in secret; and thy Father which seeth in secret shall reward thee openly. —Matthew 6:6 (KJV)

Which has been a bigger temptation for you lately: to hide your faith under a rock, or to put your faith on display for your own glory?

20 _____ _____

_____

_____

_____

20 _____ _____

_____

_____

_____

20 _____ _____

_____

_____

_____

20 _____ _____

_____

_____

_____

20 _____ _____

_____

_____

_____

July

Hereby know we that we dwell in him, and he in us, because he hath given us of his Spirit. —1 John 4:13 (KJV)

What circumstances might feel different if you remember that, as a child of God, you are in Him and He is in you?

20 ___ _____

_____

_____

_____

20 ___ _____

_____

_____

_____

20 ___ _____

_____

_____

_____

20 ___ _____

_____

_____

_____

20 ___ _____

_____

_____

_____

July

A gossip betrays a confidence, but a trustworthy person keeps a secret. —*Proverbs 11:13 (NIV)*

How has gossip hurt your relationships?

20 _____ _____

_____

_____

20 _____ _____

_____

_____

20 _____ _____

_____

_____

20 _____ _____

_____

_____

_____

20 _____ _____

_____

_____

_____

July

Now the Lord is that Spirit: and where the Spirit of the Lord is, there is liberty. —2 Corinthians 3:17 (KJV)

Is there anything holding you back from full freedom in Christ?

20 ____ _____

_____

_____

_____

20 ____ _____

_____

_____

_____

20 ____ _____

_____

_____

_____

20 ____ _____

_____

_____

_____

20 ____ _____

_____

_____

_____

July

Being confident of this very thing, that he which hath begun a good work in you will perform it until the day of Jesus Christ . . .
—*Philippians 1:6 (KJV)*

How do you see God working in your heart?

20 _____ _____

_____

_____

20 _____ _____

_____

_____

20 _____ _____

_____

_____

20 _____ _____

_____

_____

20 _____ _____

_____

_____

July

6

In whom we have boldness and access with confidence by the faith of him. —Ephesians 3:12 (KJV)

Write a bold prayer.

20 _____ _____

_____

_____

_____

20 _____ _____

_____

_____

_____

20 _____ _____

_____

_____

_____

20 _____ _____

_____

_____

_____

20 _____ _____

_____

_____

_____

July

He giveth power to the faint; and to them that have no might he increaseth strength. —Isaiah 40:29 (KJV)

In what ways is your own strength failing?

20 _____ _____

_____

_____

_____

20 _____ _____

_____

_____

_____

20 _____ _____

_____

_____

_____

20 _____ _____

_____

_____

_____

20 _____ _____

_____

_____

_____

July

There hath no temptation taken you but such as is common to man: but God is faithful, who will not suffer you to be tempted above that ye are able; but will with the temptation also make a way to escape, that ye may be able to bear it. —1 Corinthians 10:1³ (KJV)

What temptations are you facing?

20 _____ _____

_____

_____

_____

20 _____ _____

_____

_____

_____

20 _____ _____

_____

_____

_____

20 _____ _____

_____

_____

_____

20 _____ _____

_____

_____

_____

9

July

Hear counsel, and receive instruction, that thou mayest be wise in thy latter end. —Proverbs 19:20 (KJV)

Who in your life is giving you good counsel or instruction?

20 _____ _____

_____

_____

_____

20 _____ _____

_____

_____

_____

20 _____ _____

_____

_____

_____

20 _____ _____

_____

_____

_____

20 _____ _____

_____

_____

_____

July

10

For all flesh is as grass, and all the glory of man as the flower of grass. The grass withereth, and the flower thereof falleth away: But the word of the Lord endureth for ever. And this is the word which by the gospel is preached unto you. —1 Peter 1:24–25 (KJV)

What are you pursuing most in life? Is it something eternal or something temporary?

20 _____ _____

_____

_____

_____

20 _____ _____

_____

_____

_____

20 _____ _____

_____

_____

_____

20 _____ _____

_____

_____

_____

20 _____ _____

_____

_____

_____

July

I will sing unto the LORD, because he hath dealt bountifully with me.
—Psalm 13:6 (KJV)

List some ways God has dealt bountifully with you.

20 _____ _____

_____

_____

_____

20 _____ _____

_____

_____

_____

20 _____ _____

_____

_____

_____

20 _____ _____

_____

_____

_____

20 _____ _____

_____

_____

_____

July

12

If any of you lacks wisdom, let him ask God, who gives generously to all without reproach, and it will be given him. —James 1:5 (ESV)

In what circumstance do you need God's wisdom?

20 _____ _____

_____

_____

_____

20 _____ _____

_____

_____

_____

20 _____ _____

_____

_____

_____

20 _____ _____

_____

_____

_____

20 _____ _____

_____

_____

_____

July

For I will pour water upon him that is thirsty, and floods upon the dry ground: I will pour my spirit upon thy seed, and my blessing upon thine offspring . . . —Isaiah 44:3 (KJV)

What parts of your life need to be watered by God's spirit?

20 _____ _____

_____

_____

_____

20 _____ _____

_____

_____

_____

20 _____ _____

_____

_____

_____

20 _____ _____

_____

_____

_____

20 _____ _____

_____

_____

_____

July

14

God setteth the solitary in families: he bringeth out those which are bound with chains: but the rebellious dwell in a dry land. —Psalm 68:6 (KJV)

Are you experiencing loneliness, or are you craving freedom? What is God saying to you through this verse?

20 _____ _____

_____

_____

_____

20 _____ _____

_____

_____

_____

20 _____ _____

_____

_____

_____

20 _____ _____

_____

_____

_____

20 _____ _____

_____

_____

_____

July

The Lord God is my strength, and he will make my feet like hinds' feet, and he will make me to walk upon mine high places.
—Habakkuk 3:19a (KJV)

How are you experiencing God's strength?

20 _____ _____

_____

_____

_____

20 _____ _____

_____

_____

_____

20 _____ _____

_____

_____

_____

20 _____ _____

_____

_____

_____

20 _____ _____

_____

_____

_____

July

16

I will call upon the Lord, who is worthy to be praised: so shall I be saved from mine enemies. —Psalm 18:3 (KJV)

List some reasons why God is worthy to be praised.

20 _____ _____

_____

_____

_____

20 _____ _____

_____

_____

_____

20 _____ _____

_____

_____

_____

20 _____ _____

_____

_____

_____

20 _____ _____

_____

_____

_____

July

The crucible is for silver, and the furnace is for gold, and the Lord tests hearts. —Proverbs 17:3 (ESV)

What struggles or hardships have been refining your heart?

20 _____ _____

_____

_____

20 _____ _____

_____

_____

20 _____ _____

_____

_____

20 _____ _____

_____

_____

20 _____ _____

_____

_____

_____

July

18

Blessed are the peacemakers: for they shall be called the children of God. —Matthew 5:9 (KJV)

In what ways are you making peace?

20 _____ _____

_____

_____

20 _____ _____

_____

_____

20 _____ _____

_____

_____

20 _____ _____

_____

_____

20 _____ _____

_____

_____

19

July

Blessed is the man that endureth temptation: for when he is tried, he shall receive the crown of life, which the Lord hath promised to them that love him. —James 1:12 (KJV)

How do you feel about the temptations you are facing?

20 _____ _____

_____

_____

_____

20 _____ _____

_____

_____

_____

20 _____ _____

_____

_____

_____

20 _____ _____

_____

_____

_____

20 _____ _____

_____

_____

_____

July

20

Let the words of my mouth, and the meditation of my heart, be acceptable in thy sight, O LORD, my strength, and my redeemer.
—Psalm 19:14 (KJV)

Write a prayer asking God to revamp any part of your thought life or emotional life that need His cleansing and healing touch.

20 _____ _____
_____
_____
_____

20 _____ _____
_____
_____
_____

20 _____ _____
_____
_____
_____

20 _____ _____
_____
_____
_____

20 _____ _____
_____
_____
_____

July

21

In the fear of the Lord is strong confidence: and his children shall have a place of refuge. —Proverbs 14:26 (KJV)

Why can you be confident, according to the Bible?

20 _____ _____

_____

_____

_____

20 _____ _____

_____

_____

_____

20 _____ _____

_____

_____

_____

20 _____ _____

_____

_____

_____

20 _____ _____

_____

_____

_____

July

22

When I said, My foot slippeth; thy mercy, O LORD, held me up.
—Psalm 94:18 (KJV)

How have you experienced mercy?

20 _____ _____

_____

_____

_____

20 _____ _____

_____

_____

_____

20 _____ _____

_____

_____

_____

20 _____ _____

_____

_____

_____

20 _____ _____

_____

_____

_____

July

23

But I have trusted in thy mercy; my heart shall rejoice in thy salvation. —Psalm 13:5 (KJV)

Are you trusting in God's mercy and rejoicing, or are you struggling with condemnation?

20____ _____

_____

_____

20____ _____

_____

_____

20____ _____

_____

_____

20____ _____

_____

_____

20____ _____

_____

_____

July

24

The heavens declare the glory of God; and the firmament sheweth his handywork. —Psalm 19:1 (KJV)

How have you seen God through His creation lately?

20 _____ _____

_____

_____

20 _____ _____

_____

_____

20 _____ _____

_____

_____

20 _____ _____

_____

_____

20 _____ _____

_____

_____

July

25

O send out thy light and thy truth: let them lead me; let them bring me unto thy holy hill, and to thy tabernacles. —Psalm 43:3 (KJV)

In what situations do you need God's light and leading?

20 _____ _____

_____

_____

_____

20 _____ _____

_____

_____

_____

20 _____ _____

_____

_____

_____

20 _____ _____

_____

_____

_____

20 _____ _____

_____

_____

_____

July

26

For this God is our God for ever and ever: he will be our guide even unto death. —Psalm 48:14 (KJV)

Looking back, how has God guided you over the last year?

20 _____ _____

_____

_____

20 _____ _____

_____

_____

20 _____ _____

_____

_____

20 _____ _____

_____

_____

20 _____ _____

_____

_____

_____

July

If ye abide in me, and my words abide in you, ye shall ask what ye will, and it shall be done unto you. —John 15:7 (KJV)

How are you abiding in God?

20 _____ _____

_____

_____

20 _____ _____

_____

_____

20 _____ _____

_____

_____

20 _____ _____

_____

_____

20 _____ _____

_____

_____

July

And he saith unto them, Follow me, and I will make you fishers of men. And they straightway left their nets, and followed him.
—Matthew 4:19-20 (KJV)

Have you let go of anything of value to follow Jesus?

20 _____ _____

_____

_____

_____

20 _____ _____

_____

_____

_____

20 _____ _____

_____

_____

_____

20 _____ _____

_____

_____

_____

20 _____ _____

_____

_____

_____

29

July

I will love thee, O Lord, my strength. —Psalm 18:1 (KJV)

What does loving God look like?

20 _____ _____

_____

_____

_____

20 _____ _____

_____

_____

_____

20 _____ _____

_____

_____

_____

20 _____ _____

_____

_____

_____

20 _____ _____

_____

_____

_____

30

July

Ye are the salt of the earth: but if the salt have lost his savour, wherewith shall it be salted? it is thenceforth good for nothing, but to be cast out, and to be trodden under foot of men. —Matthew 5:13 (KJV)

Salt is a preservative as well as a spice. How does this verse apply to your life now?

20 _____ _____

_____

_____

_____

20 _____ _____

_____

_____

_____

20 _____ _____

_____

_____

_____

20 _____ _____

_____

_____

_____

20 _____ _____

_____

_____

_____

July

Some trust in chariots, and some in horses: but we will remember the name of the LORD our God. —Psalm 20:7 (KJV)

What are you trusting in?

20 _____ _____

_____

_____

20 _____ _____

_____

_____

20 _____ _____

_____

_____

20 _____ _____

_____

_____

20 _____ _____

_____

_____

1

August

Let your light so shine before men, that they may see your good works, and glorify your Father which is in heaven. —Matthew 5:16 (KJV)

How is your light shining?

20 _____ _____

_____

_____

_____

20 _____ _____

_____

_____

_____

20 _____ _____

_____

_____

_____

20 _____ _____

_____

_____

_____

20 _____ _____

_____

_____

_____

August

As the hart panteth after the water brooks, so panteth my soul after thee, O God. —Psalm 42:1 (KJV)

Are you thirsting more for God or for other things, people, or experiences?

20 _____ _____

_____

_____

_____

20 _____ _____

_____

_____

_____

20 _____ _____

_____

_____

_____

20 _____ _____

_____

_____

_____

20 _____ _____

_____

_____

_____

August

Therefore if thou bring thy gift to the altar, and there rememberest that thy brother hath ought against thee; Leave there thy gift before the altar, and go thy way; first be reconciled to thy brother, and then come and offer thy gift. —Matthew 5:23–24 (KJV)

Is there someone you need to reconcile with? What's your first step?

20 _____ _____

_____

_____

_____

20 _____ _____

_____

_____

_____

20 _____ _____

_____

_____

_____

20 _____ _____

_____

_____

_____

20 _____ _____

_____

_____

_____

August

4

In God we boast all the day long, and praise thy name for ever. Selah. —Psalm 44:8 (KJV)

Do you ever boast about God? What does that look like?

20 ___ _____

_____

_____

_____

20 ___ _____

_____

_____

_____

20 ___ _____

_____

_____

_____

20 ___ _____

_____

_____

_____

20 ___ _____

_____

_____

_____

August

5

Forgive us our debts, as we also forgive our debtors. —Matthew 6:12 (WEB)

Ask God to show you any unforgiveness in your heart. What makes it hard to let go of that debt? Write a prayer asking for God's help.

20 _____ _____

_____

_____

_____

20 _____ _____

_____

_____

_____

20 _____ _____

_____

_____

_____

20 _____ _____

_____

_____

_____

20 _____ _____

_____

_____

_____

August

Keep your tongue from evil and your lips from speaking deceit.
—Psalm 34:13 (ESV)

Are your words truthful and honoring to God?

20 _____ _____

_____

_____

_____

20 _____ _____

_____

_____

_____

20 _____ _____

_____

_____

_____

20 _____ _____

_____

_____

_____

20 _____ _____

_____

_____

_____

August

Therefore, whatever you desire for men to do to you, you shall also do to them; for this is the law and the prophets. —Matthew 7:12 (KJV)

Sometimes the "golden rule" is hardest to follow with our families or closest friends. Are you treating those closest to you the way you want to be treated?

20 ____ _____

_____

_____

20 ____ _____

_____

_____

_____

20 ____ _____

_____

_____

_____

20 ____ _____

_____

_____

_____

20 ____ _____

_____

_____

_____

August

*. . . if my people who are called by my name humble themselves,
and pray and seek my face and turn from their wicked ways, then I
will hear from heaven and will forgive their sin and heal their land.*
—2 Chronicles 7:14 (ESV)

How might you need to humble yourself?

20 _____ _____

_____

_____

_____

20 _____ _____

_____

_____

_____

20 _____ _____

_____

_____

_____

20 _____ _____

_____

_____

_____

20 _____ _____

_____

_____

_____

August

9

What I tell you in the darkness, speak in the light; and what you hear whispered in the ear, proclaim on the housetops. —Matthew 10:27 (WEB)

Are you taking time in Scripture and prayer to hear what God is whispering? Is there anything He's asking you to share?

20 _____ _____

_____

_____

20 _____ _____

_____

_____

20 _____ _____

_____

_____

20 _____ _____

_____

_____

20 _____ _____

_____

_____

_____

August

A fool takes no pleasure in understanding, but only in expressing his opinion. —Proverbs 18:2 (ESV)

Reflect on this verse and write your thoughts.

20 ___ _____

_____

_____

20 ___ _____

_____

_____

_____

20 ___ _____

_____

_____

_____

20 ___ _____

_____

_____

_____

20 ___ _____

_____

_____

_____

August

But let justice roll on like rivers, and righteousness like a mighty stream. —Amos 5:24 (WEB)

Are you longing for justice in some area? Write a prayer about it.

20 ___ _____

_____

_____

20 ___ _____

_____

_____

20 ___ _____

_____

_____

20 ___ _____

_____

_____

20 ___ _____

_____

_____

August

He has told you, O man, what is good; and what does the LORD require of you but to do justice, and to love kindness, and to walk humbly with your God? —Micah 6:8 (ESV)

Are you lacking justice, kindness, or humility in your life?

20 _____ _____

_____

_____

20 _____ _____

_____

_____

20 _____ _____

_____

_____

20 _____ _____

_____

_____

20 _____ _____

_____

_____

August

13

Open your mouth for the mute, for the rights of all who are destitute. Open your mouth, judge righteously, defend the rights of the poor and needy. —Proverbs 31:8–9 (ESV)

What can you do today to follow these commands?

20 _____ _____

_____

_____

_____

20 _____ _____

_____

_____

_____

20 _____ _____

_____

_____

_____

20 _____ _____

_____

_____

_____

20 _____ _____

_____

_____

_____

14

August

You will not fear the terror of the night, nor the arrow that flies by day, nor the pestilence that stalks in darkness, nor the destruction that wastes at noonday. —Psalm 91:5–6 (ESV)

In what areas do you need to trust God?

20 _____ _____

_____

_____

_____

20 _____ _____

_____

_____

_____

20 _____ _____

_____

_____

_____

20 _____ _____

_____

_____

_____

20 _____ _____

_____

_____

_____

15

August

This is my comfort in my affliction, that your promise gives me life
—Psalm 119:50 (ESV)

What are some of God's life-giving promises?

20 _____ _____

_____

_____

20 _____ _____

_____

_____

20 _____ _____

_____

_____

20 _____ _____

_____

_____

20 _____ _____

_____

_____

_____

August

16

Fear not, for I am with you; be not dismayed, for I am your God; I will strengthen you, I will help you, I will uphold you with my righteous right hand. —Isaiah 41:10 (ESV)

How have you experienced God's help lately?

20 ___ _____

_____

_____

_____

20 ___ _____

_____

_____

_____

20 ___ _____

_____

_____

_____

20 ___ _____

_____

_____

_____

20 ___ _____

_____

_____

_____

August

These things I have spoken unto you, that in me ye might have peace. In the world ye shall have tribulation: but be of good cheer; I have overcome the world. —John 16:33 (KJV)

Do you often experience joy and peace in the midst of tough circumstances? Why or why not?

20 ___ _____

_____

_____

_____

20 ___ _____

_____

_____

_____

20 ___ _____

_____

_____

_____

20 ___ _____

_____

_____

_____

20 ___ _____

_____

_____

_____

August

Lead me in your truth and teach me, for you are the God of my salvation; for you I wait all the day long. —Psalm 25:5 (ESV)

In what specific areas do you need God's leading and teaching?

20 _____ _____

_____

_____

_____

20 _____ _____

_____

_____

_____

20 _____ _____

_____

_____

_____

20 _____ _____

_____

_____

_____

20 _____ _____

_____

_____

_____

August

19

The purpose in a man's heart is like deep water, but a man of understanding will draw it out. —Proverbs 20:5 (ESV)

In what ways might you need to take action to fulfill the purpose God has given you?

20 _____ _____

_____

_____

20 _____ _____

_____

_____

20 _____ _____

_____

_____

20 _____ _____

_____

_____

20 _____ _____

_____

_____

_____

August

Therefore will not we fear, though the earth be removed, and though the mountains be carried into the midst of the sea . . .
—*Psalm 46:2 (KJV)*

When anxiety creeps in, what are some practical ways you can lean in to God's love and strength?

20 _____ _____

_____

_____

_____

20 _____ _____

_____

_____

_____

20 _____ _____

_____

_____

_____

20 _____ _____

_____

_____

_____

20 _____ _____

_____

_____

_____

August

Though the fig tree should not blossom, nor fruit be on the vines, the produce of the olive fail and the fields yield no food . . . yet I will rejoice in the LORD; I will take joy in the God of my salvation.
—Habakkuk 3:17–18 (ESV)

Write your own version of this verse with whatever "failures" you're experiencing and how you will respond to God in the midst of them.

20 _____ _____

_____

_____

_____

20 _____ _____

_____

_____

_____

20 _____ _____

_____

_____

_____

20 _____ _____

_____

_____

_____

20 _____ _____

_____

_____

_____

August

But when they looked up, they saw that the stone, which was very large, had been rolled away. —Mark 16:4 (NIV)

What "large stone" do you need miraculously rolled away?

20 _____ _____

_____

_____

_____

20 _____ _____

_____

_____

_____

20 _____ _____

_____

_____

_____

20 _____ _____

_____

_____

_____

20 _____ _____

_____

_____

_____

23

August

Thou art my hiding place; thou shalt preserve me from trouble; thou shalt compass me about with songs of deliverance. Selah.
—Psalm 32:7 (KJV)

Write a "song of deliverance" that God is putting in your heart. It could be an actual song or hymn, or just something that comes to mind.

20 _____ _____

_____

_____

_____

20 _____ _____

_____

_____

_____

20 _____ _____

_____

_____

_____

20 _____ _____

_____

_____

_____

20 _____ _____

_____

_____

_____

August

Three times I pleaded with the Lord about this, that it should leave me. But he said to me, "My grace is sufficient for you, for my power is made perfect in weakness." Therefore I will boast all the more gladly of my weaknesses, so that the power of Christ may rest upon me. —2 Corinthians 12:8–9 (ESV)

What weakness in your life is God using to display His power?

20 _____ _____

_____

_____

20 _____ _____

_____

_____

20 _____ _____

_____

_____

20 _____ _____

_____

_____

20 _____ _____

_____

_____

25

August

Being justified freely by his grace through the redemption that is in Christ Jesus . . . —Romans 3:24 (KJV)

Are you still trying to earn your redemption, or are you humbly accepting the gift of grace?

20_____ _____

_____

_____

_____

20_____ _____

_____

_____

_____

20_____ _____

_____

_____

_____

20_____ _____

_____

_____

_____

20_____ _____

_____

_____

_____

August

26

"No one can serve two masters, for either he will hate the one and love the other, or else he will be devoted to one and despise the other. You can't serve both God and Mammon." —*Matthew 6:24 (WEB)*

Who or what are you serving? How do you know?

20 _____ _____

_____

_____

20 _____ _____

_____

_____

20 _____ _____

_____

_____

20 _____ _____

_____

_____

_____

20 _____ _____

_____

_____

_____

August

I will make thy name to be remembered in all generations: therefore shall the people praise thee for ever and ever. —Psalm 45:17 (KJV)

How is your life making God's name known?

20 _____ _____

_____

_____

_____

20 _____ _____

_____

_____

_____

20 _____ _____

_____

_____

_____

20 _____ _____

_____

_____

_____

20 _____ _____

_____

_____

_____

August

28

As each has received a gift, use it to serve one another, as good stewards of God's varied grace . . . —1 Peter 4:10 (ESV)

How are you serving others with your gifts?

20_____ _____

_____

_____

20_____ _____

_____

_____

20_____ _____

_____

_____

20_____ _____

_____

_____

_____

20_____ _____

_____

_____

_____

29

August

All these with one accord were devoting themselves to prayer, together with the women and Mary the mother of Jesus, and his brothers. —Acts 1:14 (ESV)

Who do you pray with regularly?

20 _____ _____

_____

_____

20 _____ _____

_____

_____

20 _____ _____

_____

_____

20 _____ _____

_____

_____

20 _____ _____

_____

_____

_____

August

30

I therefore, a prisoner for the Lord, urge you to walk in a manner worthy of the calling to which you have been called, with all humility and gentleness, with patience, bearing with one another in love . . . —Ephesians 4:1–2 (ESV)

In what ways is (or isn't) your life marked by humility, gentleness, patience, and forbearance?

20 _____ _____

_____

_____

_____

20 _____ _____

_____

_____

_____

20 _____ _____

_____

_____

_____

20 _____ _____

_____

_____

_____

20 _____ _____

_____

_____

_____

August

31

And though a man might prevail against one who is alone, two will withstand him—a threefold cord is not quickly broken.
—Ecclesiastes 4:12 (ESV)

Who do you have standing with you in prayer, fellowship, and accountability?

20 _____ _____

_____

_____

_____

20 _____ _____

_____

_____

_____

20 _____ _____

_____

_____

_____

20 _____ _____

_____

_____

_____

20 _____ _____

_____

_____

_____

September

Love is patient and kind; love does not envy or boast; it is not arrogant . . . —1 Corinthians 13:4 (ESV)

Write a prayer asking the Holy Spirit to help you love well.

20 _____ _____

_____

_____

20 _____ _____

_____

_____

20 _____ _____

_____

_____

20 _____ _____

_____

_____

20 _____ _____

_____

_____

September

2

Many waters can't quench love, neither can floods drown it . . .
—Song of Solomon 8:7 (WEB)

What human relationship has given you a taste of God's unquenchable love for you?

20 _____ _____

_____

_____

_____

20 _____ _____

_____

_____

_____

20 _____ _____

_____

_____

_____

20 _____ _____

_____

_____

_____

20 _____ _____

_____

_____

_____

September

3

So we have come to know and to believe the love that God has for us. God is love, and whoever abides in love abides in God, and God abides in him. —1 John 4:16 (ESV)

What does it look like to abide in God's love?

20 _____ _____

_____

_____

20 _____ _____

_____

_____

20 _____ _____

_____

_____

20 _____ _____

_____

_____

20 _____ _____

_____

_____

4

September

Above all, keep loving one another earnestly, since love covers a multitude of sins. —1 Peter 4:8 (ESV)

Loving well doesn't mean avoiding conflict or ignoring sin, but it does mean forgiving. What situation or relationship can you apply this verse to?

20 _____ _____

_____

_____

20 _____ _____

_____

_____

_____

20 _____ _____

_____

_____

_____

20 _____ _____

_____

_____

_____

20 _____ _____

_____

_____

_____

September

This is my commandment, That ye love one another, as I have loved you. —John 15:12 (KJV)

Write some ways that God has shown love to you. Is there someone God is asking you to love in any of those ways?

20 _____ _____

_____

_____

_____

20 _____ _____

_____

_____

_____

20 _____ _____

_____

_____

_____

20 _____ _____

_____

_____

_____

20 _____ _____

_____

_____

_____

September

6

Let's consider how to provoke one another to love and good works . . . —Hebrews 10:24 (WEB)

How can you inspire others to do good today?

20 _____ _____

_____

_____

20 _____ _____

_____

_____

20 _____ _____

_____

_____

20 _____ _____

_____

_____

20 _____ _____

_____

_____

September

Love one another with brotherly affection. Outdo one another in showing honor. —Romans 12:10 (ESV)

Is there someone you're always comparing yourself to? How could you bless or honor that person?

20 _____ _____

_____

_____

_____

20 _____ _____

_____

_____

_____

20 _____ _____

_____

_____

_____

20 _____ _____

_____

_____

_____

20 _____ _____

_____

_____

_____

September

What then shall we say to these things? If God is for us, who can be against us? —Romans 8:31 (ESV)

Do you feel like someone is against you? How does this verse shift your perspective?

20 _____ _____

_____

_____

20 _____ _____

_____

_____

20 _____ _____

_____

_____

20 _____ _____

_____

_____

20 _____ _____

_____

_____

_____

September

9

For great is his steadfast love toward us, and the faithfulness of the Lord endures forever. Praise the Lord! —Psalm 117:2 (ESV)

How has God been steadfast in His love for you?

20 _____ _____

_____

_____

_____

20 _____ _____

_____

_____

_____

20 _____ _____

_____

_____

_____

20 _____ _____

_____

_____

_____

20 _____ _____

_____

_____

_____

September

Let the wise hear and increase in learning, and the one who understands obtain guidance . . . —Proverbs 1:5 (ESV)

How are you learning and receiving good guidance?

20 _____ _____

_____

_____

_____

20 _____ _____

_____

_____

_____

20 _____ _____

_____

_____

_____

20 _____ _____

_____

_____

_____

20 _____ _____

_____

_____

_____

As the Father has loved me, so have I loved you. Abide in my love.
—John 15:9 (ESV)

How are you abiding in God's love?

20 _____ _____

_____

_____

20 _____ _____

_____

_____

20 _____ _____

_____

_____

20 _____ _____

_____

_____

20 _____ _____

_____

_____

September

Who shall separate us from the love of Christ? Shall tribulation, or distress, or persecution, or famine, or nakedness, or danger, or sword? —Romans 8:35 (ESV)

How does this verse speak to you?

20 _____ _____

_____

_____

_____

20 _____ _____

_____

_____

_____

20 _____ _____

_____

_____

_____

20 _____ _____

_____

_____

_____

20 _____ _____

_____

_____

_____

September

But God, being rich in mercy, because of the great love with which he loved us, even when we were dead in our trespasses, made us alive together with Christ—by grace you have been saved . . .
—Ephesians 2:4–5 (ESV)

Imagine for a moment that God had not made a way for us to come alive together with Christ. Write your thoughts or a prayer.

20 _____ _____

_____

_____

20 _____ _____

_____

_____

20 _____ _____

_____

_____

20 _____ _____

_____

_____

20 _____ _____

_____

_____

September

If we say we have no sin, we deceive ourselves, and the truth is not in us. —1 John 1:8 (ESV)

Are you deceiving yourself, or are you regularly recognizing sin in your life and asking forgiveness?

20 _____ _____

_____

_____

20 _____ _____

_____

_____

20 _____ _____

_____

_____

20 _____ _____

_____

_____

20 _____ _____

_____

_____

September

And Jesus said unto them, I am the bread of life: he that cometh to me shall never hunger; and he that believeth on me shall never thirst. —John 6:35 (KJV)

How has Jesus met your needs?

20 _____ _____

_____

_____

20 _____ _____

_____

_____

20 _____ _____

_____

_____

20 _____ _____

_____

_____

20 _____ _____

_____

_____

September

16

Delight thyself also in the LORD: and he shall give thee the desires of thine heart. —Psalm 37:4 (KJV)

What are your heart's desires?

20 ___ _____

_____

_____

20 ___ _____

_____

_____

20 ___ _____

_____

_____

20 ___ _____

_____

_____

20 ___ _____

_____

_____

September

The thief comes only to steal and kill and destroy. I came that they may have life and have it abundantly. —John 10:10 (ESV)

In what ways are you experiencing abundant life?

20 _____ _____

_____

_____

20 _____ _____

_____

_____

_____

20 _____ _____

_____

_____

20 _____ _____

_____

_____

_____

20 _____ _____

_____

_____

_____

September

"Pray therefore that the Lord of the harvest will send out laborers into his harvest." —Matthew 9:38 (WEB)

Write a brief prayer inspired by this verse.

20 _____ _____

_____

_____

20 _____ _____

_____

_____

20 _____ _____

_____

_____

20 _____ _____

_____

_____

20 _____ _____

_____

_____

September

But godliness with contentment is great gain . . . —1 Timothy 6:6 (ESV)

How can you practice contentment today?

20 ___ _____

_____

_____

20 ___ _____

_____

_____

20 ___ _____

_____

_____

20 ___ _____

_____

_____

20 ___ _____

_____

_____

September

"In all things I gave you an example, that so laboring you ought to help the weak, and to remember the words of the Lord Jesus, that he himself said, 'It is more blessed to give than to receive.'" —Acts 20:35 (WEB)

Who can you give something meaningful to today? It could be time, money, a smile, or anything else the Holy Spirit is prompting you to give.

20 _____ _____

_____

_____

_____

20 _____ _____

_____

_____

_____

20 _____ _____

_____

_____

_____

20 _____ _____

_____

_____

_____

20 _____ _____

_____

_____

_____

September

There is no fear in love; but perfect love casts out fear, because fear has punishment. He who fears is not made perfect in love. —1 John 4:18 (WEB)

What are you afraid of?

20 _____ _____

_____

_____

_____

20 _____ _____

_____

_____

_____

20 _____ _____

_____

_____

_____

20 _____ _____

_____

_____

_____

20 _____ _____

_____

_____

_____

September

22

He said to them, "Beware! Keep yourselves from covetousness, for a man's life doesn't consist of the abundance of the things which he possesses." —Luke 12:15 (WEB)

How can you stop wanting what others have?

20 _____ _____

_____

_____

20 _____ _____

_____

_____

20 _____ _____

_____

_____

20 _____ _____

_____

_____

20 _____ _____

_____

_____

September

23

There is nothing better for a person than that he should eat and drink and find enjoyment in his toil. This also, I saw, is from the hand of God . . . —Ecclesiastes 2:24 (ESV)

How can you find enjoyment in hard work?

20 _____ _____

_____

_____

_____

20 _____ _____

_____

_____

_____

20 _____ _____

_____

_____

_____

20 _____ _____

_____

_____

_____

20 _____ _____

_____

_____

_____

September

24

But you are a chosen race, a royal priesthood, a holy nation, a people for his own possession, that you may proclaim the excellencies of him who called you out of darkness into his marvelous light. —1 Peter 2:9 (ESV)

What would it look like for you to proclaim God's excellence this week?

20 _____ _____

_____

_____

_____

20 _____ _____

_____

_____

_____

20 _____ _____

_____

_____

_____

20 _____ _____

_____

_____

_____

20 _____ _____

_____

_____

_____

25

September

As for the rich in this present age, charge them not to be haughty, nor to set their hopes on the uncertainty of riches, but on God, who richly provides us with everything to enjoy. —1 Timothy 6:17 (ESV)

Reflect on how earthly riches can come and go, but hope in God is certain.

20 _____ _____

_____

_____

20 _____ _____

_____

_____

20 _____ _____

_____

_____

20 _____ _____

_____

_____

20 _____ _____

_____

_____

September

26

I know how to be brought low, and I know how to abound. In any and every circumstance, I have learned the secret of facing plenty and hunger, abundance and need. —Philippians 4:12 (ESV)

In what ways is this true—or not so true—of you?

20 _____ _____

_____

_____

_____

20 _____ _____

_____

_____

_____

20 _____ _____

_____

_____

_____

20 _____ _____

_____

_____

_____

20 _____ _____

_____

_____

_____

September

For the sake of Christ, then, I am content with weaknesses, insults, hardships, persecutions, and calamities. For when I am weak, then I am strong. —2 Corinthians 12:10 (ESV)

How are you experiencing Christ's strength as a result of your own weakness?

20 _____ _____

_____

_____

20 _____ _____

_____

_____

20 _____ _____

_____

_____

20 _____ _____

_____

_____

20 _____ _____

_____

_____

September

28

Let love be genuine. Abhor what is evil; hold fast to what is good.
—Romans 12:9 (ESV)

What are some ways you have experienced genuine love?

20 _____ _____

_____

_____

_____

20 _____ _____

_____

_____

_____

20 _____ _____

_____

_____

_____

20 _____ _____

_____

_____

_____

20 _____ _____

_____

_____

_____

September

29

The lions may grow weak and hungry, but those who seek the LORD lack no good thing. —Psalm 34:10 (NIV)

How are you seeking the Lord?

20 _____ _____

_____

_____

20 _____ _____

_____

_____

20 _____ _____

_____

_____

20 _____ _____

_____

_____

20 _____ _____

_____

_____

September

30

"But seek first his kingdom and his righteousness, and all these things will be given to you as well." —Matthew 6:33 (NIV)

How are you seeking God's kingdom?

20 _____ _____

_____

_____

20 _____ _____

_____

_____

20 _____ _____

_____

_____

20 _____ _____

_____

_____

20 _____ _____

_____

_____

October

1

Satisfy us in the morning with your steadfast love, that we may rejoice and be glad all our days. —Psalm 90:14 (ESV)

What are some examples of God's steadfast love in Scripture or in your life?

20 _____ _____

_____

_____

_____

20 _____ _____

_____

_____

_____

20 _____ _____

_____

_____

_____

20 _____ _____

_____

_____

_____

20 _____ _____

_____

_____

_____

2

October

Thanks be to God through Jesus Christ our Lord! So then, I myself serve the law of God with my mind, but with my flesh I serve the law of sin. —Romans 7:25 (ESV)

Are there situations or relationships in which you want to do the right thing but keep failing?

20 _____ _____

_____

_____

_____

20 _____ _____

_____

_____

_____

20 _____ _____

_____

_____

_____

20 _____ _____

_____

_____

_____

20 _____ _____

_____

_____

_____

3

October

For my yoke is easy, and my burden is light. —Matthew 11:30 (KJV)

What makes walking with Jesus "easy" and "light"?

20 _____ _____

_____

_____

20 _____ _____

_____

_____

20 _____ _____

_____

_____

20 _____ _____

_____

_____

20 _____ _____

_____

_____

4

October

A tranquil heart gives life to the flesh, but envy makes the bones rot. —Proverbs 14:30 (ESV)

How can you let go of envy?

20 _____ _____

_____

_____

20 _____ _____

_____

_____

20 _____ _____

_____

_____

20 _____ _____

_____

_____

20 _____ _____

_____

_____

October

My soul shall be satisfied as with marrow and fatness; and my mouth shall praise thee with joyful lips . . . —Psalm 63:5 (KJV)

When do you experience the deepest satisfaction for your soul?

20 _____ _____

_____

_____

20 _____ _____

_____

_____

20 _____ _____

_____

_____

20 _____ _____

_____

_____

20 _____ _____

_____

_____

October

6

Verily, verily, I say unto you, Except a corn of wheat fall into the ground and die, it abideth alone: but if it die, it bringeth forth much fruit. —John 12:24 (KJV)

How does this verse speak to your current experience?

20 _____ _____

_____

_____

_____

20 _____ _____

_____

_____

_____

20 _____ _____

_____

_____

_____

20 _____ _____

_____

_____

_____

20 _____ _____

_____

_____

_____

October

He that hath no rule over his own spirit is like a city that is broken down, and without walls. —Proverbs 25:28 (KJV)

Are you lacking self-control in some area?

20 _____ _____

_____

_____

20 _____ _____

_____

_____

20 _____ _____

_____

_____

20 _____ _____

_____

_____

20 _____ _____

_____

_____

October

Beloved, never avenge yourselves, but leave it to the wrath of God, for it is written, "Vengeance is mine, I will repay, says the Lord."
—Romans 12:19 (ESV)

Are you longing for vengeance? How is that affecting you?

20 ___ _____

_____

_____

_____

20 ___ _____

_____

_____

_____

20 ___ _____

_____

_____

_____

20 ___ _____

_____

_____

_____

20 ___ _____

_____

_____

_____

October

Whoever is slow to anger is better than the mighty, and he who rules his spirit than he who takes a city. —Proverbs 16:32 (ESV)

What is your relationship with anger? Does it rule you?

20 _____ _____

_____

_____

20 _____ _____

_____

_____

20 _____ _____

_____

_____

20 _____ _____

_____

_____

20 _____ _____

_____

_____

10

October

A man's heart deviseth his way: but the LORD directeth his steps.
—Proverbs 16:9 (KJV)

When has God changed your plans or redirected your steps?

20 _____ _____

_____

_____

20 _____ _____

_____

_____

20 _____ _____

_____

_____

20 _____ _____

_____

_____

20 _____ _____

_____

_____

October

11

When I am afraid, I will put my trust in you. —Psalm 56:3 (WEB)

What are you most afraid of?

20 _____ _____

_____

_____

20 _____ _____

_____

_____

20 _____ _____

_____

_____

20 _____ _____

_____

_____

_____

20 _____ _____

_____

_____

_____

October

Many are the plans in the mind of a man, but it is the purpose of the LORD that will stand. —Proverbs 19:21 (ESV)

How has God's purpose played out through interrupted plans in your life?

20 _____ _____

_____

_____

_____

20 _____ _____

_____

_____

_____

20 _____ _____

_____

_____

_____

20 _____ _____

_____

_____

_____

20 _____ _____

_____

_____

_____

October

The Lord your God is in your midst, a mighty one who will save; he will rejoice over you with gladness; he will quiet you by his love; he will exult over you with loud singing. —Zephaniah 3:17 (ESV)

What feelings does this verse bring up?

20 _____ _____

_____

_____

20 _____ _____

_____

_____

20 _____ _____

_____

_____

20 _____ _____

_____

_____

20 _____ _____

_____

_____

October

14

Set a watch, O Lᴏʀᴅ, before my mouth; keep the door of my lips.
—Psalm 141:3 (KJV)

How have your words helped or hurt others lately?

20 _____ _____

_____

_____

_____

20 _____ _____

_____

_____

_____

20 _____ _____

_____

_____

_____

20 _____ _____

_____

_____

_____

20 _____ _____

_____

_____

_____

October

I form the light, and create darkness: I make peace, and create evil: I the LORD do all these things. —Isaiah 45:7 (KJV)

What does this verse make you feel?

20 _____ _____

_____

_____

20 _____ _____

_____

_____

20 _____ _____

_____

_____

20 _____ _____

_____

_____

20 _____ _____

_____

_____

16

October

. . . and may the Lord make you increase and abound in love for one another and for all, as we do for you . . . —1 Thessalonians 3:12 (ESV)

Write a prayer asking God to increase your love for specific people in your life.

20 _____ _____

_____

_____

20 _____ _____

_____

_____

20 _____ _____

_____

_____

20 _____ _____

_____

_____

20 _____ _____

_____

_____

October

17

The fear of the LORD is the beginning of knowledge: but fools despise wisdom and instruction. —Proverbs 1:7 (KJV)

How have you been corrected or instructed lately? How did it feel?

20 _____ _____

_____

_____

_____

20 _____ _____

_____

_____

_____

20 _____ _____

_____

_____

_____

20 _____ _____

_____

_____

_____

20 _____ _____

_____

_____

_____

October

18

But when he saw the multitudes, he was moved with compassion for them because they were harassed and scattered, like sheep without a shepherd. —Matthew 9:36 (WEB)

Reflect on Jesus's compassion and the role compassion plays in your own life.

20 _____ _____

_____

_____

_____

20 _____ _____

_____

_____

_____

20 _____ _____

_____

_____

_____

20 _____ _____

_____

_____

_____

20 _____ _____

_____

_____

_____

October

19

Therefore encourage one another and build one another up, just as you are doing. —1 Thessalonians 5:11 (ESV)

How can you encourage a brother or sister in Christ today?

20 _____ _____

_____

_____

_____

20 _____ _____

_____

_____

_____

20 _____ _____

_____

_____

_____

20 _____ _____

_____

_____

_____

20 _____ _____

_____

_____

_____

October

Whoever restrains his words has knowledge, and he who has a cool spirit is a man of understanding. —Proverbs 17:27 (ESV)

When is it hardest for you to hold your tongue or stay cool? Write a prayer asking for God's help.

20 _____ _____

_____

_____

_____

20 _____ _____

_____

_____

_____

20 _____ _____

_____

_____

_____

20 _____ _____

_____

_____

_____

20 _____ _____

_____

_____

_____

October

21

When pride comes, then comes shame, but with humility comes wisdom. —Proverbs 11:2 (WEB)

How can you recognize and combat pride in your life?

20 _____ _____

_____

_____

20 _____ _____

_____

_____

20 _____ _____

_____

_____

20 _____ _____

_____

_____

20 _____ _____

_____

_____

_____

October

22

Behold, you desire truth in the inward parts. You teach me wisdom in the inmost place. —Psalm 51:6 (WEB)

Has God revealed any dishonesty or foolishness in your heart of hearts?

20 _____ _____

_____

_____

20 _____ _____

_____

_____

20 _____ _____

_____

_____

20 _____ _____

_____

_____

20 _____ _____

_____

_____

October

But now that you have come to know God, or rather to be known by God, why do you turn back again to the weak and miserable elemental principles, to which you desire to be in bondage all over again? —Galatians 4:9 (WEB)

Write your thoughts about this verse and where you're at in life.

20 _____ _____

_____

_____

_____

20 _____ _____

_____

_____

_____

20 _____ _____

_____

_____

_____

20 _____ _____

_____

_____

_____

20 _____ _____

_____

_____

_____

October

24

A man who isolates himself pursues selfishness, and defies all sound judgment. —Proverbs 18:1 (WEB)

How are you connecting with other believers?

20 _____ _____

_____

_____

20 _____ _____

_____

_____

20 _____ _____

_____

_____

20 _____ _____

_____

_____

20 _____ _____

_____

_____

October

25

Moses said, "Please show me your glory." —Exodus 33:18 (WEB)

Do you ever ask God to reveal more of Himself to you? How do you see God's glory?

20 _____ _____

_____

_____

_____

20 _____ _____

_____

_____

_____

20 _____ _____

_____

_____

_____

20 _____ _____

_____

_____

_____

20 _____ _____

_____

_____

_____

October

26

*He healeth the broken in heart, and bindeth up their wounds. —
Psalm 147:3 (KJV)*

How is God healing your heart?

20 _____ _____

_____

_____

_____

20 _____ _____

_____

_____

_____

20 _____ _____

_____

_____

_____

20 _____ _____

_____

_____

_____

20 _____ _____

_____

_____

_____

October

Jesus said to her, "Didn't I tell you that if you believed, you would see God's glory?" —John 11:40 (WEB)

How does belief affect the way you see God and worship Him?

20___ _____

_____

_____

20___ _____

_____

_____

_____

20___ _____

_____

_____

20___ _____

_____

_____

20___ _____

_____

_____

_____

October

Yours, O LORD, is the greatness and the power and the glory and the victory and the majesty, for all that is in the heavens and in the earth is yours. Yours is the kingdom, O LORD, and you are exalted as head above all. —1 Chronicles 29:11 (ESV)

What are you praising God for?

20 _____ _____

_____

_____

_____

20 _____ _____

_____

_____

_____

20 _____ _____

_____

_____

_____

20 _____ _____

_____

_____

_____

20 _____ _____

_____

_____

_____

October

. . . for you were bought with a price. So glorify God in your body.
—1 Corinthians 6:20 (ESV)

How can you glorify God in your body?

20 _____ _____

_____

_____

20 _____ _____

_____

_____

_____

20 _____ _____

_____

_____

_____

20 _____ _____

_____

_____

_____

20 _____ _____

_____

_____

_____

October

Therefore welcome one another as Christ has welcomed you, for the glory of God. —Romans 15:7 (ESV)

How are you welcoming others, or how have you been welcomed?

20 _____ _____

_____

_____

_____

20 _____ _____

_____

_____

_____

20 _____ _____

_____

_____

_____

20 _____ _____

_____

_____

_____

20 _____ _____

_____

_____

_____

October

31

As he sat in the house, behold, many tax collectors and sinners came and sat down with Jesus and his disciples. When the Pharisees saw it, they said to his disciples, "Why does your teacher eat with tax collectors and sinners?" —Matthew 9:10–11 (WEB)

Who are you building relationships with outside of your circle of believing friends and family?

20 _____ _____

_____

_____

_____

20 _____ _____

_____

_____

_____

20 _____ _____

_____

_____

_____

20 _____ _____

_____

_____

_____

20 _____ _____

_____

_____

_____

November

Whatever you ask in my name, this I will do, that the Father may be glorified in the Son. —John 14:13 (ESV)

What are you asking God for?

20 _____ _____

_____

_____

_____

20 _____ _____

_____

_____

_____

20 _____ _____

_____

_____

_____

20 _____ _____

_____

_____

_____

20 _____ _____

_____

_____

_____

November

2

Not unto us, O LORD, not unto us, but unto thy name give glory, for thy mercy, and for thy truth's sake. —Psalm 115:1 (KJV)

Are you seeking God's glory more than your own?

20 _____ _____

_____

_____

_____

20 _____ _____

_____

_____

_____

20 _____ _____

_____

_____

_____

20 _____ _____

_____

_____

_____

20 _____ _____

_____

_____

_____

November

3

If it is possible, as much as it is up to you, be at peace with all men.
—Romans 12:18 (WEB)

Write a prayer about any relationship in which peace seems impossible.

20____ _____

_____

_____

20____ _____

_____

_____

20____ _____

_____

_____

20____ _____

_____

_____

20____ _____

_____

_____

November

4

Finally, brothers, rejoice. Aim for restoration, comfort one another, agree with one another, live in peace; and the God of love and peace will be with you. —2 Corinthians 13:11 (ESV)

Is there a relationship in which you need to "aim for restoration"? How might you start?

20 _____ _____

_____

_____

20 _____ _____

_____

_____

20 _____ _____

_____

_____

20 _____ _____

_____

_____

20 _____ _____

_____

_____

November

5

First of all, then, I urge that supplications, prayers, intercessions, and thanksgivings be made for all people, for kings and all who are in high positions, that we may lead a peaceful and quiet life, godly and dignified in every way. —1 Timothy 2:1–2 (ESV)

Write a prayer for those in authority in your government.

20 _____ _____

_____

_____

20 _____ _____

_____

_____

20 _____ _____

_____

_____

20 _____ _____

_____

_____

20 _____ _____

_____

_____

November

6

Let not steadfast love and faithfulness forsake you; bind them around your neck; write them on the tablet of your heart.
—Proverbs 3:3 (ESV)

Is there someone in your life God is asking you to love faithfully, even if you're getting nothing in return from them?

20 _____

_____

_____

20 _____

_____

_____

20 _____

_____

_____

20 _____

_____

_____

20 _____

_____

_____

November

Be not wise in your own eyes; fear the LORD, and turn away from evil. —Proverbs 3:7 (ESV)

What does it mean to be "wise in your own eyes"? How can you avoid that?

20 _____ _____

_____

_____

20 _____ _____

_____

_____

20 _____ _____

_____

_____

20 _____ _____

_____

_____

20 _____ _____

_____

_____

November

Count it all joy, my brothers, when you meet trials of various kinds, for you know that the testing of your faith produces steadfastness. —James 1:2–3 (ESV)

What trials are you facing and how might God be using them?

20 _____ _____

_____

_____

20 _____ _____

_____

_____

20 _____ _____

_____

_____

20 _____ _____

_____

_____

20 _____ _____

_____

_____

November

9

Rejoice in hope, be patient in tribulation, be constant in prayer.
—Romans 12:12 (ESV)

Which of these commands is hardest for you? Why?

20 _____ _____

_____

_____

_____

20 _____ _____

_____

_____

_____

20 _____ _____

_____

_____

_____

20 _____ _____

_____

_____

_____

20 _____ _____

_____

_____

_____

November

10

When Jesus came into the ruler's house and saw the flute players and the crowd in noisy disorder, he said to them, "Make room, because the girl isn't dead, but sleeping . . ." —Matthew 9:23–24 (WEB)

Is there a relationship or situation that others perceive as "dead," when maybe God is just waiting for a chance to display His life-giving power?

20 _____ _____

_____

_____

_____

20 _____ _____

_____

_____

_____

20 _____ _____

_____

_____

_____

20 _____ _____

_____

_____

_____

20 _____ _____

_____

_____

_____

November

Rejoice always, pray without ceasing, give thanks in all circumstances; for this is the will of God in Christ Jesus for you.
—*1 Thessalonians 5:16–18 (ESV)*

Why can you give thanks no matter what is happening in your life?

20 _____ _____

_____

_____

_____

20 _____ _____

_____

_____

_____

20 _____ _____

_____

_____

_____

20 _____ _____

_____

_____

_____

20 _____ _____

_____

_____

_____

November

. . . for we walk by faith, not by sight. —*2 Corinthians 5:7 (WEB)*

What situation are you trusting God with, even though you can't see the outcome?

20 _____ _____

_____

_____

_____

20 _____ _____

_____

_____

_____

20 _____ _____

_____

_____

_____

20 _____ _____

_____

_____

_____

20 _____ _____

_____

_____

_____

November

Is any among you suffering? Let him pray. Is any cheerful? Let him sing praises. —James 5:13 (WEB)

Share your heart with God through a few lines of prayer or praises.

20 _____ _____

_____

_____

_____

20 _____ _____

_____

_____

_____

20 _____ _____

_____

_____

_____

20 _____ _____

_____

_____

_____

20 _____ _____

_____

_____

_____

November

14

. . . giving thanks always concerning all things in the name of our Lord Jesus Christ, to God, even the Father . . . —Ephesians 5:20 (WEB)

When is it hardest to give thanks?

20 _____ _____

_____

_____

20 _____ _____

_____

_____

20 _____ _____

_____

_____

20 _____ _____

_____

_____

20 _____ _____

_____

_____

15

November

Therefore I tell you, whatever you ask in prayer, believe that you have received it, and it will be yours. —Mark 11:24 (ESV)

Are there certain prayers you have trouble believing will be answered? Why?

20 _____ _____

_____

_____

_____

20 _____ _____

_____

_____

_____

20 _____ _____

_____

_____

_____

20 _____ _____

_____

_____

_____

20 _____ _____

_____

_____

_____

16

November

As for you, brothers, do not grow weary in doing good. —2 Thessalonians 3:13 (ESV)

How can you combat burnout when it comes to doing good?

20 ____ _____

_____

_____

_____

20 ____ _____

_____

_____

_____

20 ____ _____

_____

_____

_____

20 ____ _____

_____

_____

_____

20 ____ _____

_____

_____

_____

November

17

Confess your faults one to another, and pray one for another, that ye may be healed. The effectual fervent prayer of a righteous man availeth much. —James 5:16 (KJV)

Who can you share your sins with? What makes that person a good accountability partner?

20 _____ _____

_____

_____

20 _____ _____

_____

_____

20 _____ _____

_____

_____

20 _____ _____

_____

_____

20 _____ _____

_____

_____

18

November

And pray in the Spirit on all occasions with all kinds of prayers and requests. With this in mind, be alert and always keep on praying for all the Lord's people. —Ephesians 6:18 (NIV)

Is there anything you feel like you can't pray about or share with God?

20 _____ _____

_____

_____

20 _____ _____

_____

_____

20 _____ _____

_____

_____

20 _____ _____

_____

_____

20 _____ _____

_____

_____

November

19

When the righteous cry for help, the Lord hears and delivers them out of all their troubles. —Psalm 34:17 (ESV)

Do you ever cry out to God for help, or are your prayers safe and polite?

20 _____ _____

_____

_____

20 _____ _____

_____

_____

20 _____ _____

_____

_____

20 _____ _____

_____

_____

20 _____ _____

_____

_____

_____

November

"Behold, I send you out as sheep among wolves. Therefore be wise as serpents and harmless as doves." —Matthew 10:16 (WEB)

How does Jesus's admonition speak to you?

20 _____ _____

_____

_____

_____

20 _____ _____

_____

_____

_____

20 _____ _____

_____

_____

_____

20 _____ _____

_____

_____

_____

20 _____ _____

_____

_____

_____

November

21

Continue steadfastly in prayer, being watchful in it with thanksgiving. —Colossians 4:2 (ESV)

Is there anything you've been praying for for a long time?

20 _____ _____

_____

_____

20 _____ _____

_____

_____

20 _____ _____

_____

_____

20 _____ _____

_____

_____

20 _____ _____

_____

_____

22

November

Let us come into his presence with thanksgiving; let us make a joyful noise to him with songs of praise! —Psalm 95:2 (ESV)

Write a verse here of your favorite song or hymn of praise.

20 _____ _____

_____

_____

20 _____ _____

_____

_____

20 _____ _____

_____

_____

20 _____ _____

_____

_____

20 _____ _____

_____

_____

23

November

Enter into his gates with thanksgiving, and into his courts with praise: be thankful unto him, and bless his name. —Psalm 100:4 (KJV)

How can you bless God's name?

20 _____ _____

_____

_____

_____

20 _____ _____

_____

_____

_____

20 _____ _____

_____

_____

_____

20 _____ _____

_____

_____

_____

20 _____ _____

_____

_____

_____

November

24

And rising very early in the morning, while it was still dark, he departed and went out to a desolate place, and there he prayed.
—Mark 1:35 (ESV)

What does it take for you to have time alone with God?

20 _____ _____

_____

_____

20 _____ _____

_____

_____

20 _____ _____

_____

_____

20 _____ _____

_____

_____

20 _____ _____

_____

_____

November

25

Praise ye the LORD: for it is good to sing praises unto our God; for it is pleasant; and praise is comely. —Psalm 147:1 (KJV)

What are you praising God for today?

20 _____ _____

_____

_____

_____

20 _____ _____

_____

_____

_____

20 _____ _____

_____

_____

_____

20 _____ _____

_____

_____

_____

20 _____ _____

_____

_____

_____

November

26

You ask and do not receive, because you ask wrongly, to spend it on your passions. —James 4:3 (ESV)

Are you asking God for anything "wrongly"?

20 _____ _____

_____

_____

20 _____ _____

_____

_____

20 _____ _____

_____

_____

20 _____ _____

_____

_____

_____

20 _____ _____

_____

_____

_____

November

27

You will be enriched in every way to be generous in every way, which through us will produce thanksgiving to God.
—2 Corinthians 9:11 (ESV)

How can you be more generous with whatever God has given you?

20 _____ _____

_____

_____

_____

20 _____ _____

_____

_____

_____

20 _____ _____

_____

_____

_____

20 _____ _____

_____

_____

_____

20 _____ _____

_____

_____

_____

November

See the birds of the sky, that they don't sow, neither do they reap, nor gather into barns. Your heavenly Father feeds them. Aren't you of much more value than they? —Matthew 6:26 (WEB)

Do you really believe you are precious to God? How does that affect your trust in Him?

20 _____ _____

_____

_____

20 _____ _____

_____

_____

20 _____ _____

_____

_____

20 _____ _____

_____

_____

20 _____ _____

_____

_____

November

29

"Until now you have asked nothing in my name. Ask, and you will receive, that your joy may be full." —John 16:24 (ESV)

What are you asking for in Jesus's name?

20 _____ _____

_____

_____

20 _____ _____

_____

_____

20 _____ _____

_____

_____

20 _____ _____

_____

_____

20 _____ _____

_____

_____

_____

November

I will praise the name of God with a song, and will magnify him with thanksgiving. —Psalm 69:30 (KJV)

What attributes of God's character are you especially thankful for?

20 _____ _____

_____

_____

_____

20 _____ _____

_____

_____

_____

20 _____ _____

_____

_____

_____

20 _____ _____

_____

_____

_____

20 _____ _____

_____

_____

_____

1

December

But let him ask in faith, with no doubting, for the one who doubts is like a wave of the sea that is driven and tossed by the wind.
—James 1:6 (ESV)

What makes you doubt?

20 _____ _____

_____

_____

20 _____ _____

_____

_____

20 _____ _____

_____

_____

20 _____ _____

_____

_____

20 _____ _____

_____

_____

December

2

Evening and morning and at noon I utter my complaint and moan, and he hears my voice. —Psalm 55:17 (ESV)

Do you trust God with your feelings? Is it ever not OK to complain to God?

20 _____ _____

_____

_____

_____

20 _____ _____

_____

_____

_____

20 _____ _____

_____

_____

_____

20 _____ _____

_____

_____

_____

20 _____ _____

_____

_____

_____

December

3

May the God of hope fill you with all joy and peace in believing, so that by the power of the Holy Spirit you may abound in hope.
—Romans 15:13 (ESV)

What role does hope play in your daily life?

20 _____ _____

_____

_____

_____

20 _____ _____

_____

_____

_____

20 _____ _____

_____

_____

_____

20 _____ _____

_____

_____

_____

20 _____ _____

_____

_____

_____

December

*Praise ye the L*ORD*. O give thanks unto the L*ORD*; for he is good: for his mercy endureth for ever. —Psalm 106:1 (KJV)*

How have you experienced God's mercy?

20 ____ _____

_____

_____

_____

20 ____ _____

_____

_____

_____

20 ____ _____

_____

_____

_____

20 ____ _____

_____

_____

_____

20 ____ _____

_____

_____

_____

December

And whenever you stand praying, forgive, if you have anything against anyone, so that your Father also who is in heaven may forgive you your trespasses. —Mark 11:25 (ESV)

Is there anyone you need to forgive?

20 _____ _____

_____

_____

_____

20 _____ _____

_____

_____

_____

20 _____ _____

_____

_____

_____

20 _____ _____

_____

_____

_____

20 _____ _____

_____

_____

_____

6

December

Praise ye him, sun and moon: praise him, all ye stars of light.
—Psalm 148:3 (KJV)

How does it feel to know you are joining with all God's creation in praising Him?

20 _____ _____

_____

_____

_____

20 _____ _____

_____

_____

_____

20 _____ _____

_____

_____

_____

20 _____ _____

_____

_____

_____

20 _____ _____

_____

_____

_____

December

. . . casting all your anxieties on him, because he cares for you.
—1 Peter 5:7 (ESV)

How do you know God cares for you?

20 _____ _____

_____

_____

_____

20 _____ _____

_____

_____

_____

20 _____ _____

_____

_____

_____

20 _____ _____

_____

_____

_____

20 _____ _____

_____

_____

_____

December

8

By him therefore let us offer the sacrifice of praise to God continually, that is, the fruit of our lips giving thanks to his name.
—Hebrews 13:15 (KJV)

How is praise a sacrifice?

20 _____ _____

_____

_____

_____

20 _____ _____

_____

_____

_____

20 _____ _____

_____

_____

_____

20 _____ _____

_____

_____

_____

20 _____ _____

_____

_____

_____

December

9

Let them praise your great and awesome name! Holy is he!
—Psalm 99:3 (ESV)

Write your own psalm praising God for who He is.

20 _____ _____

_____

_____

_____

20 _____ _____

_____

_____

_____

20 _____ _____

_____

_____

_____

20 _____ _____

_____

_____

_____

20 _____ _____

_____

_____

_____

December

He said to them, "Why are you fearful, O you of little faith?" Then he got up, rebuked the wind and the sea, and there was a great calm.
—Matthew 8:26 (WEB)

What is Jesus saying to you in the midst of whatever storms you're facing?

20 _____ _____

_____

_____

20 _____ _____

_____

_____

20 _____ _____

_____

_____

_____

20 _____ _____

_____

_____

_____

20 _____ _____

_____

_____

_____

December

Oh give thanks to the LORD, for he is good; for his steadfast love endures forever! —Psalm 118:29 (ESV)

How has God's love been steadfast toward you?

20 _____ _____

_____

_____

20 _____ _____

_____

_____

20 _____ _____

_____

_____

20 _____ _____

_____

_____

20 _____ _____

_____

_____

_____

December

Rather, speaking the truth in love, we are to grow up in every way into him who is the head, into Christ . . . —Ephesians 4:15 (ESV)

When has someone spoken the truth in love to you? How is that different from speaking the truth without love?

20 _____ _____

_____

_____

_____

20 _____ _____

_____

_____

_____

20 _____ _____

_____

_____

_____

20 _____ _____

_____

_____

_____

20 _____ _____

_____

_____

_____

December

My mouth will tell of your righteous acts, of your deeds of salvation all the day, for their number is past my knowledge.
—Psalm 71:15 (ESV)

What are some of God's righteous acts?

20____ _____

_____

_____

_____

20____ _____

_____

_____

_____

20____ _____

_____

_____

_____

20____ _____

_____

_____

_____

20____ _____

_____

_____

_____

14

December

Little children, let us not love in word or talk but in deed and in truth. —1 John 3:18 (ESV)

How can you love in deed and in truth today?

20 ____ _____

_____

_____

20 ____ _____

_____

_____

_____

20 ____ _____

_____

_____

_____

20 ____ _____

_____

_____

_____

20 ____ _____

_____

_____

_____

December

Therefore, having put away falsehood, let each one of you speak the truth with his neighbor, for we are members one of another.
—Ephesians 4:25 (ESV)

When are you most tempted to gossip or stretch the truth?

20_____ _____

_____

_____

_____

20_____ _____

_____

_____

_____

20_____ _____

_____

_____

_____

20_____ _____

_____

_____

_____

20_____ _____

_____

_____

_____

December

But Mary treasured up all these things, pondering them in her heart. —Luke 2:19 (ESV)

What moments or experiences are you treasuring up in your heart? What are you pondering?

20 ___ _____

_____

_____

_____

20 ___ _____

_____

_____

_____

20 ___ _____

_____

_____

_____

20 ___ _____

_____

_____

_____

20 ___ _____

_____

_____

_____

December

Let us therefore celebrate the festival, not with the old leaven, the leaven of malice and evil, but with the unleavened bread of sincerity and truth. —1 Corinthians 5:8 (ESV)

How are you practicing sincerity and truth?

20 _____ _____

_____

_____

_____

20 _____ _____

_____

_____

_____

20 _____ _____

_____

_____

_____

20 _____ _____

_____

_____

_____

20 _____ _____

_____

_____

_____

December

18

For by grace you have been saved through faith. And this is not your own doing; it is the gift of God, not a result of works, so that no one may boast. —Ephesians 2:8–9 (ESV)

How would you describe God's grace to someone who doesn't know Him?

20 _____ _____

_____

_____

_____

20 _____ _____

_____

_____

_____

20 _____ _____

_____

_____

_____

20 _____ _____

_____

_____

_____

20 _____ _____

_____

_____

_____

December

19

But if it is by grace, it is no longer on the basis of works; otherwise grace would no longer be grace. —Romans 11:6 (ESV)

What motivates your good works?

20 _____ _____

_____

_____

_____

20 _____ _____

_____

_____

_____

20 _____ _____

_____

_____

_____

20 _____ _____

_____

_____

_____

20 _____ _____

_____

_____

_____

December

But God shows his love for us in that while we were still sinners, Christ died for us. —Romans 5:8 (ESV)

What does this verse remind you about who God is?

20 _____ _____

_____

_____

_____

20 _____ _____

_____

_____

_____

20 _____ _____

_____

_____

_____

20 _____ _____

_____

_____

_____

20 _____ _____

_____

_____

_____

December

But grow in the grace and knowledge of our Lord and Savior Jesus Christ. To him be the glory both now and to the day of eternity. Amen. —2 Peter 3:18 (ESV)

In what ways is your faith growing?

20 _____ _____

_____

_____

_____

20 _____ _____

_____

_____

_____

20 _____ _____

_____

_____

_____

20 _____ _____

_____

_____

_____

20 _____ _____

_____

_____

_____

December

. . . for he who is mighty has done great things for me, and holy is his name. —Luke 1:49 (ESV)

This is part of Mary's song of praise, often called Mary's Magnificat. What great things has God done for you?

20 _____ _____

_____

_____

_____

20 _____ _____

_____

_____

_____

20 _____ _____

_____

_____

_____

20 _____ _____

_____

_____

_____

20 _____ _____

_____

_____

_____

23

December

And let the peace of Christ rule in your hearts, to which indeed you were called in one body. And be thankful. —Colossians 3:15 (ESV)

Is Christ's peace ruling in your heart?

20 _____ _____

_____

_____

20 _____ _____

_____

_____

20 _____ _____

_____

_____

20 _____ _____

_____

_____

20 _____ _____

_____

_____

December

And the Word was made flesh, and dwelt among us, (and we beheld his glory, the glory as of the only begotten of the Father,) full of grace and truth. —John 1:14 (KJV)

The creator of the universe humbled Himself to live in the confines of a human body amongst sinners of all kinds. How might that give perspective to a challenging relationship, or with whom you choose to spend time?

20 _____ _____

_____

_____

_____

20 _____ _____

_____

_____

_____

20 _____ _____

_____

_____

_____

20 _____ _____

_____

_____

_____

20 _____ _____

_____

_____

_____

December

25

Thanks be to God for his inexpressible gift! —2 Corinthians 9:15 (ESV)

Write a prayer of thanksgiving and praise for the inexpressible gift of His Son.

20 _____ _____

_____

_____

_____

20 _____ _____

_____

_____

_____

20 _____ _____

_____

_____

_____

20 _____ _____

_____

_____

_____

20 _____ _____

_____

_____

_____

December

26

Oh give thanks to the LORD; call upon his name; make known his deeds among the peoples! —1 Chronicles 16:8 (ESV)

How do you talk about God's deeds when you're with other people?

20 _____ _____

_____

_____

_____

20 _____ _____

_____

_____

_____

20 _____ _____

_____

_____

_____

20 _____ _____

_____

_____

_____

20 _____ _____

_____

_____

_____

December

Therefore let us be grateful for receiving a kingdom that cannot be shaken, and thus let us offer to God acceptable worship, with reverence and awe . . .—Hebrews 12:28 (ESV)

How would you describe your worship?

20 _____ _____

_____

_____

_____

20 _____ _____

_____

_____

_____

20 _____ _____

_____

_____

_____

20 _____ _____

_____

_____

_____

20 _____ _____

_____

_____

_____

28

December

....

Blessed be the Lord, who daily bears us up; God is our salvation. Selah —Psalm 68:19 (ESV)

How do you need God to hold you up and support you today?

20 _____ _____

_____

_____

_____

20 _____ _____

_____

_____

_____

20 _____ _____

_____

_____

_____

20 _____ _____

_____

_____

_____

20 _____ _____

_____

_____

_____

December

29

Have nothing to do with irreverent, silly myths. Rather train yourself for godliness; for while bodily training is of some value, godliness is of value in every way, as it holds promise for the present life and also for the life to come. —1 TImothy 4:7–8

How are you training yourself for godliness?

20 _____ _____

_____

_____

20 _____ _____

_____

_____

20 _____ _____

_____

_____

20 _____ _____

_____

_____

20 _____ _____

_____

_____

_____

December

30

Hearken unto the voice of my cry, my King, and my God: for unto thee will I pray. —Psalm 5:2 (KJV)

How does it affect your prayers to know that God is your King?

20 ___ _____

_____

_____

_____

20 ___ _____

_____

_____

_____

20 ___ _____

_____

_____

_____

20 ___ _____

_____

_____

_____

20 ___ _____

_____

_____

_____

December

31

. . . who saved us and called us to a holy calling, not because of ou works but because of his own purpose and grace, which he gave u in Christ Jesus before the ages began . . . —2 Timothy 1:9 (ESV)

What is your purpose?

20_____ _____

20_____ _____

20_____ _____

20_____ _____

20_____ _____